THE
STRATEGY
OF COMBAT

WAR TODAY
East versus West

THE STRATEGY OF COMBAT

ARCO PUBLISHING, INC.
New York

CONTENTS

Editor Nigel Flynn
Designer Gordon Robertson

Published 1985 by
Arco Publishing, Inc.
215 Park Avenue South
New York, NY 10003

Original material ©Eshel Dramit Limited,
Israel 1983. All rights reserved.
Reproduction in whole or part
without permission forbidden.
This arrangement Marshall Cavendish
Limited 1985.

Library of Congress Cataloging in Publication Data

Main entry under title:

The Strategy of combat.

(War today – East vs. West)
1. Europe – Military policy. 2. United States –
Military policy. 3. Biological warfare – Europe.
4. Chemical warfare – Europe. I. Series.
UA646.S76 1985 355'.03304 85-3851
ISBN 0-668-06519-2
ISBN 0-668 06523-0 (pbk.)

Printed in Spain by Jerez Industrial, S. A.

INTRODUCTION

The world today is alive to the danger of nuclear war. In almost every part of the globe the USSR and the USA are more or less in open conflict. Neither side is prepared to make the slightest concession to the other. Both have vast vested interests maintained by an ever-expanding military machine that makes a mockery of talk about arms control and détente.

US foreign policy is based on the grim determination to hold on to every inch of territory and every sphere of influence built up over the past 30 years. To the present adminstration, the threat of communism — real or imagined — is sufficient to launch massive military strikes in almost any part of the world.

And for their part, the Russians are committed to the destruction of capitalism — at least in theory. In reality they are motivated by self-interest in the same way as the USA, and are almost as dependent upon capitalism as the Americans are.

In the world of superpower politics the manufacture and deployment of nuclear weapons is just one element in a dangerous game being played out every day on the world's stage.

And the trump card is the sale of arms to the 'uncommitted' countries of the Third World. To persuade these countries to buy arms they don't need, massive sums of money have been invested by both East and West in the form of economic 'aid'. And the lure of untold riches has been a temptation few have been able to resist. Consequently, considerable parts of the globe have become little more than the testing ground for a new and terrifying destruction.

Most awesome in this arsenal is the threat now posed by a new generation of chemical and biological agents. Evidence is accumulating that both powers are using, have used, or are supplying to their allies, chemical and biological weapons: the Americans in Vietnam, the Russians in Afghanistan.

The weapons manufactured for today's chemical and biological warfare (CBW) have come a long way since they were first used on the battlefields of Europe during World War 1. Both superpowers now hold such vast stocks of sophisticated compounds that, unleashed, yet new vistas of horror would open in the long history of human suffering. Civilian populations would be the first victims of such warfare. Given the virulence of the micro-organisms used in today's biological bombs, and the toxicity of the latest nerve gases, there is little protection for the populations exposed to them.

But another — and more heartening — aspect of the current crisis between East and West is the growing refusal by ordinary men and women to accept that the escalation of the arms race is unstoppable. Peace movements in every European nation are taking to the streets to demonstrate passionate opposition to the threat of war. In the pages that follow, the strength and the arguments of the peace movements are assessed.

At the end of the day, the weapons and hazards of modern warfare are too important to be left to the devices and decisions of either politicians or professional military men. What is needed, many feel, is a new understanding of what war means — nothing less than a new science and a new 'sociology' of war.

Fine minds in strong bodies

Above Soviet officer cadets present arms. They will form the Red Army's top men of tomorrow.

Down the years, as times have changed, the Soviet Union and the United States have perfected their systems of command. Nothing is left to chance in the pursuit of ultimate efficiency. The humblest pawn on the world's chessboard is moved by a powerful machine, protected from all risk. This is how the credibility of the two greatest armies in the world is assessed.

Above Cadets at West Point in the United States, seed-bed of future American strategy.

THE SOVIET UNION

If US defence policy is more or less open to public scrutiny, it is quite another matter in the Soviet Union. It is very difficult to disentangle the mechanisms that bind the armed forces together, the systems of communication and the relationships between the men in the military hierarchy. Open debates like those that take place in the US Congress are unthinkable in Russia.

To add to these difficulties, it is impossible to study Soviet military command and the organisation of its armed forces without taking into consideration the existence of the Warsaw Pact. Not only is the USSR the only nuclear power in the Pact, it also accounts for 60 per cent of the forces in the front line.

However, the Warsaw Pact is not an organisation of command in time of war: its main purpose is to act as an administrative organisation and to train troops. Soviet forces are deployed in the central part of Eastern Europe and are generally made up of some thirty divisions. These forces are organised into four groups which, in the event of war, would be deployed according to instructions from the Soviet High Command.

The military organisation of the Warsaw Pact is made up of a unified high command which is responsibile for the management and co-ordination of the various armed forces. This high command is led by the commander-in-chief of the armed forces and includes a military council – a system modelled upon the one that exists in the Soviet Union. The council assembles under the presidency of the chief of staff and the military representatives of non-Soviet forces.

The Warsaw Pact has no air defence organisation as such, but it can call on the national Soviet system, known as PVO-Strany. A deputy commander of this organisation is commander of the air forces in Eastern Europe. He is also in charge of six principal networks which are properly Soviet, including long-range warning systems, radar, attack and interception forces as well as ground-to-air missiles.

The Soviet Union also controls the local air forces of the Warsaw Pact countries, which are, however, responsible for the defence of their own air space.

Soviet representatives work in each capital in direct communication with the unified high command and are responsible for co-ordinating intelligence work and the supervision of operations. Finally, a technical committee oversees the supply of arms, the stocking of military equipment and the improvement of standard logistic installations. It also supervises the armament industries of Eastern Europe.

History of the Red Army

The army is an important power in the life of every Soviet citizen; a dynamic, living reality. It has a great hold over the population and forms an essential framework for the running of the country.

This complex organization, which extends its influence to the life of every person, did not appear by chance. The Red Army was born in 1917 from the ashes of the Tsarist army. At the outset, the new army was controlled purely by 'soviets' of ordinary soldiers. The result was chaos. From 1918, as the mists of idealism began to clear, it was

Above Russian guardsmen goose-stepping in Red Square.

Leon Trotsky who took matters firmly in hand. Results were swift. In a matter of months, the army was strong enough to hurl several million men against Poland.

The 'esprit de corps' that obtained in the new-style military machine was something of a revelation to the world at large. What distinguished the Red Army from any other in history was the dominant position enjoyed by its so-called 'commissars'. Under the new system, officers were now considered to be merely specialists in a particular field of activity – it was the commissar's authority that counted. This new breed of disciplinarian – civilians though they were – had tight control over both officers and men.

However, the army was largely demobilised between 1925 and 1930 and was reconstituted in a form that allowed the traditional officer class a measure of 'rehabilitation'. Even something akin to an old-style 'officer corps' began to emerge again – with all the trappings of promotion, rank, honour and high levels of pay.

The arrival of Stalin at the helm swiftly dealt a mortal blow to the military hierarchy. Stalin purged the high command with drastic effect. In the following years, he established his control over the Soviet army, with disastrous results when the Germans invaded in 1941. It was only after

Above The annual parade of military might on the anniversary of the Revolution.

1943 that the world became aware of the formidable might of the Soviet military machine.

The Army

The Soviet forces are composed of two main bodies, the army and the navy, both under the command of the Ministry of Defence. The army is considered as the more important of the two, national defence being its main concern. It is made up of two parts: ground forces and air forces.

The ground forces are divided into armies, corps and divisions. In peace time, the principal commands are those of the military regions and those of the army groups and the armies stationed in the other Warsaw Pact countries. In time of war, the armies would come under the tactical command and the administrative direction of the headquarters of the different fronts.

The air forces are divided into air armies. Each is made up of three army corps formed from several aerial divisions, which include three air regiments. These forces are divided between those protecting Soviet territory and those used for tactical operations or for penetration over long distances. The latter are attached to the Ministry of Defence while the tactical groups are under the orders of the military administration or the army groups.

To protect Russian territory from enemy aircraft or missiles there is an anti-aircraft defence organization called the PVO (National Air Defence Troops). It is divided into home anti-aircraft defence and anti-aircraft defence of the armed forces. The aim of the former is to protect the population, industrial centres, lines of communication – the whole infrastructure. This is the PVO's most important job.

To facilitate this task, the air force puts at the PVO's and the C-in-C's disposal the following hardware: fighters for air defence (IAPVO), sufficient anti-aircraft units, artillery, regiments and battalions of personnel specialising in signals, defence against chemical warfare, military engineering and construction.

All these systems at the PVO's disposal are organised into anti-aircraft defence regions and are principally deployed to protect obvious targets of enemy attack.

Anti-aircraft defence forces are generally made up from the other military groups. The command and general staff posts are held predominantly by infantry officers. There are also non-commissioned officers from the artillery and the air force.

In time of war air and ground forces and air defence will be integrated at the Theatres of Military Operations (TVD) level.

ДА ЗДРАВСТВУЕТ МИРОЛЮБИВАЯ, ЛЕНИНСКАЯ ВНЕШНЯЯ ПОЛИТИКА СОВЕТСКОГО СОЮЗА!
ВОПЛОТИМ В ЖИЗНЬ СОВЕТСКУЮ ПРОГРАММУ МИРА!
ВСЕ СИЛЫ — НА БОРЬБУ ЗА МИР!
СЛАВА
КРАСНАЯ ПРЕСНЯ
ЛЕНИНСКИЙ

The face of Russian communism today: *Left* May Day, Moscow 1983. *Above* A grim faced soldier looks on.

The Navy

The Soviet fleet's autonomy, as opposed to the Army's, dates to over forty years ago. In 1937 a commissariat for the Navy was created which had responsibility for the administration and general deployment of the fleet during the course of the second stage of its development.

Nevertheless, during the whole of World War 2, the Soviet fleet was just a back-up to the Army. The commissariat of both Navy and Army were integrated at the beginning of 1946 into a single Ministry of the Armed Forces, the Navy thus losing a little more of its autonomy.

It was not until 1950 that autonomy was regained by the creation of a separate Ministry for the Navy. In March 1953, the ministries of the Army and the Navy were again amalgamated to form the Ministry of Defence. The Navy is thus independent of the Army, but belongs to the same ministry.

A permanent framework

Apart from the two main military bodies, there are two paramilitary organizations – the armed forces attached to the Ministry of the Interior (MVD) and Committee for State Security (KGB), both of which have a more political stance.

These paramilitary forces allow the regime to keep a firm hold on the nation. Thus, in the event of a military coup, the government could call on devoted and loyal assistance to assure its defence. Several million people work full- or part-time for the security forces of the MDV or the KGB. These forces encompass the secret police, the militia, the firemen, civil defence services and thousands of informers.

About one million military personnel are employed full-time. Even though their recruitment is carried out by the Ministry of Defence, it is in fact subject to the orders of the Council of Ministers. As an intermediary the Council uses the KGB, since it is above the MVD in the administrative hierarchy.

There also exists a civilian organization with a military bias known as the Association of Volunteers for Co-operation with the Army, the Airforce and the Navy (DOSAAF). Its aim is to contribute to the formation and military preparation of civilian groups. The DOSAAF is organized on a national level. It prepares the population for civil defence and is active throughout the country through various associations of independent status such as clubs and meetings in factories, collective farms, and so on.

The DOSAAF also has a programme of military training – firearms practise, parachute jumping, sailing, horse-riding – along with more unusual skills such as use of chemical weapons and anti-aircraft defence. Its duties also involve collaboration with the league of young communists, called the Komsomol.

The commanding officers of the Association of Volunteers for Co-operation with the army are usually retired military personnel or reserve officers. All the equipment used by the volunteers is donated by the army. It is important to realize that in the event of general mobilization, the DOSAAF would present itself as a force trained for armed service and capable of responding to varied demands. Members of DOSAAF could be used as snipers or as part of a sabotage crew.

There is no maximum age limit for entry to the Volunteers' Association, but a minimum limit of 15 years is in force.

'You will be an officer, my son . . .'

As in every army in the world the effectiveness of the Soviet military machine depends, in the final analysis, on the quality of its fighting men. Every citizen in the Soviet Union has his or her part to play in the vast military complex created by the communist state. And for those destined to become professional soldiers, their careers are carefully mapped out for them.

The future soldier first joins the Young Pioneers. This organization – which some have likened to the Boy Scouts in Britain – is in fact a paramilitary group preparing the young communist for the rigours of military life. It does have its lighter side, however, and since its creation in the 1920s it has offered opportunities for relaxation, social events and summer holidays for the underprivileged members of the Soviet state.

At the age of 12 the Young Pioneer begins his preparation for the army: learning to handle small arms, shoot and carry out simple troop manoeuvres. At 15, the would-be soldier has been absorbed into the DOSAAF, or, for those in the cities, joined one of the military classes as part of his normal secondary education. And the summer holidays are spent at obligatory military camps drilling, marching and practising small arms firing.

For those who show promise there is a rigorous selection procedure for officer cadetship. Those who succeed go directly to an officer's training school to complete their secondary education. And for those who have not the stuff to make an officer but wish to be professional soldiers, there are special schools for potential NCOs.

Above A crack unit of Soviet paratroopers armed with the *Kalashnikov* rifle.

Suvorov academies

Named after the Russian general, these specialised schools for officers were created during World War 2 when the abysmal quality of the officer corps made it imperative to establish a new kind of training that incorporated an acceptable level of education.

Pupils at the Suvorov academies are aged between 10 to 13 when they are admitted and are boarders. The course lasts five to seven years, according to the academic level the pupil had reached before admission. Classical subjects are taught in every college, as well as military history, army regulations, small arms training, driving vehicles and politics.

Upon completion of the course, graduates may enter university, but they always remain on call-up to the army as members of the reserve force. Most, however, prefer to enter military life straightaway, in which case they attend a college for officers.

Colleges for officers

Courses in these colleges last from two to three years, according to which branch of the armed forces is selected. Each college is under the administrative command of the military region in which it is situated. Most colleges specialize in preparing officers for infantry, artillery or armour.

Candidates entering these colleges all have to be between 18 and 23 years of age, to have above average intelligence and to be politically impeccable. Graduates are commissioned with the rank of second lieutenant in the arm of their choice.

Colleges of Higher Education for Officers

These colleges are designed for subalterns already serving with field force units and aim to perfect them in their chosen specialism. Students can follow intensive courses which enables them to become teachers themselves, or choose a more difficult option with the aim of obtaining positions of command. Each of the services and each branch has its college of higher education.

Voroshilov institutes of higher military education

Diplomas obtained from the Colleges of Higher Education for Officers enables officers to enter the Voroshilov Institute for higher military studies. If students manage to graduate from this last centre of instruction, they have a good chance of becoming senior officers.

Conscription

Military service is obligatory in the Soviet Union. Everybody physically fit must serve some time in one of the armed forces. Young people have to sign on at their local recruitment office at the beginning of their 18th year. Every male judged fit for service can be called to the colours.

Men assigned to the infantry normally serve two years. Those who prefer a more specialized branch are enrolled for three years. The system is similar to that in Western Europe, even if the organization is not identical. The course comprises a period of formal instruction and two periods of training, one in winter and the other in summer.

In the event of conflict, the Soviet Union would proceed to general mobilization, progressively incorporating all the registrants of the recruiting offices from that year and from those preceding it. Those with a preparatory military training would immediately be placed in reserve units and sent to the front if necessary.

Re-organization

Throughout 1983 and early 1984, Western intelligence agencies received reports and rumours of major organizational changes within the Soviet armed forces. Though details of these changes remain vague, and are likely to do so, it is possible to piece together the available information into a fairly coherent picture. And the picture makes gloomy reading for strategists in the West.

The most important change has been the creation of three 'theatres': Western, Southern and Far Eastern, together with a Central Reserve area comprising the Moscow, Volga and Ural Military districts. In the event of war these theatres will be reinforced by Operational Manoeuvre Groups – all-arms mobile forces intended to exploit any weakness in NATO defences and to penetrate rear areas as deeply and as quickly as possible, disrupting communications, blocking the movement of reinforcements.

The Soviet air force has also been streamlined. It now comprises 20 Regional Commands and 5 Air Armies. The 10 air defence districts have now been reduced to five.

These changes, together with other attempts at reducing the top-heavy bureaucracy, has made the Soviet military machine a more flexible and capable fighting force.

Above US sailors show the flag at the American base at San Diego.

THE UNITED STATES

The American war effort is a perfectly oiled machine which is set in motion by the Secretary of Defense through several agencies.

The Defense Department is the most bureacratic political body in the USA. It consumes vast amounts of money but is still the most efficient system in the world. Americans often accuse this 'branch' of government of draining away too much of the nation's resources. Some do not like their money spent on the Pentagon, the largest employer in North America.

Even so, Americans are proud of their defence system, especially since the election of Ronald Reagan. It is the sign of a great nation, a fact that gives them a marked sense of identity.

The Department of Defense was created in 1947 by the National Security Act. It was preceded by a military body divided into a Department of War and a Department of the Navy. Today, after 30 years of modification, the Pentagon is split into five distinct departments: the Office of the Secretary of Defense (OSD), combined headquarters of the Joint Chiefs of Staff (JCS), the departments of the three armed forces, the Defense Agencies and the operational commands.

It is impossible to describe the Pentagon without mentioning one of the principal bodies responsible for the organization of defence: Congress.

The Commander-in-Chief of the Armed Forces is Ronald Reagan, President of the United States. He delegates authority to the Secretary of Defense, who controls the Pentagon. His position carries enormous responsibilities. In the first place, the Secretary of Defense has to administer and direct the organization of defence, its resources and the units that comprise it.

Besides this, he is responsible for controlling all the operations of the armed forces, and, lastly, he has to advise the President on all aspects of national security. The Secretary of Defense is assisted by a deputy but the Defense Secretary's office is not limited to these two men. There are eleven assistants of equal rank and a judicial adviser. Each has his own organization to administer. Altogether, there are about 2,000 staff in the Pentagon, three-quarters of whom are civilians.

Acting as the right-hand man of the Secretary, the Deputy Secretary supervises and co-ordinates the activities of the Pentagon according to directives from above. He can thus give orders to all those units at home and abroad which are under the aegis of the Department of Defense. Budgetary problems on this level are the deputy secretary's business. He is the one who has to evaluate any proposition put to the head of the Pentagon and to satisfy himself that it fits the budget.

Today, the law permits the Secretary to have nine assistants, but does not define their precise sphere of influence. As a general rule, whatever their area of activity – equipment, international security, etc. – they must operate according to certain directives. In pursuit of this end, each has a number of assistants and an office of 150 to 200 employees. They are thus very important men, key figures

Above Bird's-eye view of the Pentagon, Washington: nerve-centre of the US military machine.

in the Pentagon hierarchy. Moreover, all of them, along with the Secretary himself and his deputy, must have their nominations approved by Senate.

As well as these nine assistants, the Defense Secretary has under him a Director of Research and Engineering for Defense (DDR&E), a Director of Control Systems, a Director of Command and Telecommunications (DDTCCS) and a General Adviser.

Combined headquarters

All the members of combined headquarters are nominated by the President and submitted to the Senate. At the heart of the Defense Department, combined headquarters (JCS) has four important functions. According to the precepts of the Council for National Security (NSC) it advises the President and the Secretary of Defense. It also has to prepare short-, medium- and long-term plans for different aspects of defence: strategy and logistics, military aid programmes, industrial mobilization, research and development, and the priorities for operational commands.

The JCS supervises the programmes and the orders of the operational commands and the armed services. It also assists the Defense Secretary and the President in applying their strategic and tactical directives. Four generals are at the head of combined headquarters: the commander-in-chief of the army, the commander of naval operations, the commander-in-chief of the air force and a president.

The latter can belong to one of the three armed forces, but he must sever his connection with that body during his term of office. When matters concerning the Marines are on the agenda, the commander of the Marines is allowed to participate in the debate, but he is not allowed to vote.

The JCS is assisted by 1,400 military personnel and 50 civilians, 400 of whom are attached to headquarters, with equal representation for the three armed forces. This unit is called the Joint Staff. Its main function is to prepare reports which the JCS can rely on when making a decision. The director of this unit is a general nominated by the president of the JCS for two years. He has to be approved by the Defense Secretary.

Departments of the three armed forces

Contrary to popular belief, the role of the three armed forces was not ordained from the beginning. The three departments – army, navy and air force – were not set up by statute nor are they as important as ministries. They act as agencies whose principal tasks are the recruitment, the training and the equipping of the armed forces.

Moreover, the authority of the departments in this sphere is only very temporary. In fact, as soon as one of the armed forces receives an operational command, it has the responsibility to see that it is carried out. Each department is directed by a secretary, who has under him an assistant secretary and an office staffed by military personnel and ten civilians, making up about 100 people in all.

Each secretary's military headquarters is divided into 15 specific sections. It is directed by the service's commander-in-chief.

Defense agencies

There is no law limiting the number of agencies serving the Pentagon. The Defense Secretary can thus create as many as he wants. Today there are eleven. They are composed of civil and military personnel, the first enjoying permanent status, the latter temporary. Their effective strength varies enormously. They average 3,000, but some have

Above Cadets at West Point take the oath of allegiance.

150 while others have 50,000. These agencies only cost the Pentagon a small amount – about 3 per cent of the total budget.

National Security Agency (NSA)
The National Security Agency is directed by a general under the control of the Defense Secretary. His role is crucial: to protect the communications of the armed forces and to intercept those of foreign countries. It is principally thanks to this agency that the United States gained intelligence about the Soviet Union's intentions regarding intervention in the Middle East in 1973.

Defense Advanced Research Projects Agency (DARPA)
The DARPA is under the control of a high-ranking official but equally subject to direction by the Defense Secretary. Its job is to maintain American supremacy in military technology. It must be able to predict the potential of any development programme or project.

Defense Nuclear Agency (DNA)
Directed by a general, the Defense Nuclear Agency is directly responsible to combined headquarters. It administers and maintains the American nuclear arms system. It also liaises between the Defense Department and other departments concerned with nuclear matters.

Defense Communications Agency (DCA)
With a general in command, the DCA is under the control of combined headquarters. It controls communications systems worldwide for the armed forces and the Pentagon. It also directs the National Communications System, and the satellite communications systems.

Defense Intelligence Agency (DIA)
This agency is in a unique position. Although it is directed by a general and attached to the Defense Secretary, it can also carry out special missions for combined headquarters. Its role is to take care of intelligence operations, and to this end it can make use of the armed forces and supervises the intelligence services attached to each department.

Defense Supply Agency (DSA)
Directly under the control of the Secretary of Defense, it is commanded by a general. The DSA controls all supplies bought by the Pentagon.

Defense Contract Audit Agency (DCAA)
This agency is commanded by a general under the control of the Secretary of Defense. It is responsible for the smooth running of the Pentagon's contracts. It is also in charge of all legal matters which may arise.

Defense Security Assistance Agency (DSAA)
The DSAA is also directed by a general under the control of the Defense Secretary. Its task is to ensure the smooth running of all foreign aid programmes and military assistance programmes. The director of the DSAA is also Under-Secretary of Defense for International Affairs.

Defense Civil Preparedness Agency (DCPA)
The DCPA is directed by a high-ranking civilian official and is concerned with civil defence programmes. It also gives aid on a local level in the event of natural disasters.

Defense Mapping Agency (DMA)
This agency is under the control of combined headquarters and commanded by a general. It is concerned with maps and topography and satellite reconnaissance.

Above An airwoman in the US Air Force.
Right Marines just after disembarking at Grenada.
Far right US Marines parade in Washington.

Defense Investigative Service (DIS)
This is the 'police force' of the armed services and the Pentagon. It is commanded by a high-ranking civilian under the control of the Secretary of Defense. It is in charge of all enquiries affecting the Pentagon and those relating to common law.

Operational commands
Operational commands are joint or specific areas of authority over the American armed forces. Those which are 'joint' are to do with geographical areas and concern at least two of the armed forces. The 'specific' ones concern one continuous mission being carried out by one branch only of the armed forces.

In fact, there are five unified joint commands. Four of them relate to specific geographical zones: the Atlantic, the Pacific, Europe and the Southern Region. The fifth is called 'Readiness Command'. It is based in the United States and made up of forces from the army and the airforce. Its role is to offer reinforcements for overseas commands. There are also three specific commands which are quite separate: the Strategic Air Command, the Aerospace Defense Command and the Military Airlift Command.

A four-star general is in charge of the unified commands. The Pacific and Atlantic Commands are directed by admirals. Those of Europe, the Southern Region and Readiness Command are the responsibility of air force generals. The three specific commands are under the direction of air force generals. The commanders-in-chief are responsible to the President and the Secretary of Defense.

The commander-in-chief of a unified command can also give orders to a specific command.

Command, control and communications (C3)
These words generally mean the totality of the system which permits the National Command Authorities, that is the President and the Secretary of Defense, effectively to command the armed forces. These three systems depend on fast execution. They include satellites, communications under the sea and on the ground, and all other forms of electronic communications. In the event of war, particularly nuclear war, it is imperative to possess reconnaissance, communications and alert systems which are immediately operational. It is the essential basis for a credible defence organization.

Combined headquarters is in charge of systems C3. It has a number of different methods for transmitting essential orders. Among these are the National Military Command System (NMCS), the National Military Command Center (NMCC), the Alternate Military Command Center (ANMCC), and the National Emergency Airborne Command Post (NEACP), in which the President might ride out a nuclear attack.

However, there are also other means of communication. First, there is the Defense Communications Systems. Although deployed in peace time, it can equally well be used in time of war for all the American units world-wide.

Under the direction of the Defense Communications Agency, the DCS is controlled directly by the overseas government. It can also be used for civilian purposes.

Other communications bodies include: the tactical level, which is divided between different units in the country, command posts, observation sectors, etc. Mobility is the key to this system.

There are other intermediate systems for the nuclear sector. Thus, the Worldwide Military Command and Control System takes care of communications between the different unified and specific commands and controls the special system for the nuclear forces. This special nuclear body, called the Minimum Essential Emergency Communications Network, offers the President and the Secretary of Defense the best possible guarantee of retaining control over the different nuclear amaments during and after a nuclear attack.

For the large units deployed all over the world, these systems assure the command, the control and the communications of the National Command Authorities. It is also important to realise that in a crisis all the organs of strategic and economic command will be assembled aboard a Boeing aircraft. This will fly at a few miles altitude and will hold the President, the Secretary of Defense, certain generals and officials from the Pentagon.

Congress

The importance of Congress on the Pentagon cannot be overlooked. When missions are transferred from one service to another, it can exercize its right of veto. Also, it is important to stress that the budgetary process is one of the most important aspects of the Pentagon's functions. In this process there are two phases: the fixing of the budget by the administration and a second period during which Congress studies the proposals and modifies them if it wishes.

These proceedings take two and a half years. Combined headquarters begins the process with a review of what it considers to be necessary. Then the Secretary of Defense oversees the detailed planning which constitutes the Pentagon's position on the composition of its future budget. The Pentagon's needs are then measured against the political realities of the administration, financial constraints and the nature of foreign politics.

Finally, after the budget has been formulated, all the propositions are submitted to the President. He has to make a decision when the points of view of the administration and the Secretary of Defense differ radically. He does so while taking into account both the USA's entire budget worldwide and the international situation.

It is here that Congress makes its appearance. It represents in effect the last stage before the President puts his signature to the document. First, it fixes the global limit to the Defense budget which is at the heart of the Federal budget. At the same time, it gives, or withholds, authorisation to the individual programmes that make up the Pentagon's budget.

After having voted on the main programmes, Congress passes a law fixing the extent of the budget worldwide. One stage of this vote on the budget is particularly spectacular. This is when the committees of the armed forces of the two assemblies conduct their examination of official personalities. Sometimes the different committees have to listen to more than a thousand witnesses. These marathons do little to speed up the proceedings! Very often, too, problems solved at the administration level come up again and have to be discussed once more.

Below American armour on manoeuvres in West Germany.

Above An NCO school in Okinawa.

In spite of all these interruptions, it is often the case that the final budget is not very different from the one fixed by Congress several months before. This long journey will nevertheless have had the merit of airing all the problems, of listening to the most informed opinion and above all, of leaving nothing to chance. It is, perhaps, the price that has to be paid for democracy.

World-wide commitments

In 1982, the US government was spending something in the region of 215,900 *million* dollars, or 7.2 per cent of the GNP, on defence. This figure, released by the International Institute for Strategic Studies, does not include money spent on defence by other ministries, money spent on the space programme with military application, money spent on research, on paramilitary organizations or indeed on the activities of the CIA. How then is the money spent?

At the beginning of 1984 the US had more military commitments on a global scale than at any time since the end of World War 2. Its army is now stretched thinly in the Far East, the Middle East, Western Europe and Central America. What this means, in military and political terms, we shall see in the section What makes Washington tick?

Airland Battle

In the battle of wits waged by the Pentagon against senior Soviet strategists, the US army now has a plan to counter any threatened invasion of Western Europe by the Warsaw Pact. It is based on an appreciation of current Soviet military tactics projected forward 20 years.

Faced with the overwhelming numerical superiority enjoyed by the Warsaw Pact, the Pentagon believes that the best form of defence is attack. Rather than meeting the Warsaw Pact in the field and fighting a war of attrition, US forces in Europe are now training for a different sort of war. Basic to the concept is the creation of small, highly-trained and flexible combat units able to fight in 360 degrees. Faced with a Soviet onslaught, these units would penetrate deep behind Soviet lines causing confusion and preventing reinforcements reaching the front. And the Soviet weakness is an inability to sustain the fight without heavy reinforcements. Thus the Americans hope to maximise their effectiveness and minimise the Soviet superiority.

THE WORLD
IN FLAMES

The planet: win or lose

Nothing happens in the world without one side seeing some sinister motive in the other. Reality or fantasy? One thing is certain. Moscow and Washington both have huge interests of every sort and are determined to protect them. The planet has become the chessboard for these privileged giants. If one moves a pawn, his opponent is not far behind. What is the basis of this rivalry?

Soldiers using Soviet weapons in Eritrea.

Above Warships of the Soviet fleet in Cuba.

What makes Moscow tick?

Clausewitz's saying 'War is the pursuit of policy by other means' aptly sums up the Soviet attitude to foreign policy. The USSR has learned to adopt a flexible response in order to maintain its influence and to exploit, wherever possible, its self-interest. In practical terms this is obviously governed by the current political situation, world wide, and an accurate assessment of what the West is up to.

In *The Armed forces of the Soviet State*, Marshal Gretchko wrote: 'Soviet military policy, above all in its military aspect, is not immutable.' To Gretchko this is the right response to a series of questions facing Soviet military strategists:

— Who will be the enemy in any future war?
— What sort of war will it be and how will the armed forces meet it?
— How should the Soviet state prepare for such a war?
— How should the war be conducted?
— What forces will be necessary and where should the military operation be directed?

To meet these needs the USSR has evolved a set of guiding principles that now dictates their response to almost every situation in the world today.

Governing principles

The developing rivalry between the USSR and the USA has, over the years, been projected by both sides as the struggle between capitalism and communism throughout the world. These two fundamentally different economic and social systems have propelled the two superpowers towards a two-pronged policy: make sure your own political convictions come out on top, and frustrate those of the other side wherever possible.

The Soviet view is clear: 'capitalism is leading the world to a nuclear catastrophe.' The view of the West is equally clear and uncompromising: 'the Soviets are prepared to risk everything – including nuclear war – in order to achieve their long-term ambition: the conversion of the world to Soviet-style communism.'

Just as NATO is seen by those in the West as the only guarantee of peace in our time, so the states of the Eastern bloc see the Warsaw Pact as defending 'peace by mustering the forces of peace and the power of the Soviet armed forces'. What then is the truth behind the propaganda?

'War anywhere'

Soviet policy aims at being able to launch an offensive, political, diplomatic, or economic, anywhere in the world in order to achieve its objectives. Foreign policy aims at maximising Soviet influence throughout the world and containing or eliminating Western influence.

The development of Soviet influence abroad takes on various guises: the granting of military and/or economic aid; sending in 'advisors'; cultural exchanges; the signing of treaties of 'co-operation'. But for the most part, the activities of these foreign missions remains secret.

Decisions concerning foreign policy are taken at Politburo level. The director of the international department of the Central Committee has to co-ordinate these decisions. Following American Defense Department practice, active measures which must remain secret are confined to the International Information Department (made up of members of the Central Committee) and to the 'A' service of the KGB (Committee for State Security).

According to US Secretary of Defense Caspar Weinberger, since 1980 the Soviets have often sown the seeds of discord between the United States and its NATO allies by the use of disinformation. This has the aim of discrediting individuals, governments or policies by the dissemination of false information.

The Soviet Union's presence in the world

The Soviet Union has woven a web covering the whole world. Its navy is present on every ocean. Its air and ground forces and 'diplomats' are implanted in every continent.

Soviet military equipment delivered to Third World countries, 1977-1982

	Total	Middle East and Southern Asia	Black Africa	Latin America	Eastern Asia and Pacific
Tanks/Mobile artillery units	7,065	5,205	1,140	80	640
Armoured vehicles	8,660	6,500	1,590	175	395
Guns (100 mm and over)	9,590	5,115	3,510	420	545
Large surface craft	32	19	5	1	7
Small surface craft	126	10	45	27	44
Naval missile launchers	53	33	4	11	8
Submarines	6	3	—	3	—
Supersonic combat aircraft	2,235	1,635	220	130	250
Subsonic combat aircraft	290	150	80	5	55
Helicopters	910	620	125	35	130
Other military planes	345	100	70	65	110
Surface-to-air missiles	11,680	9,495	1,575	435	175

Sales of military equipment 1977-1982 (in billions of dollars)

Middle East/North Africa 25.7
Black Africa 5.6
South West Asia 8.1
South Asia 3.4
South East Asia 2.2
Latin America 0.8
Cuba 1.7

Total = 47.5

Arms sales 1977-1982 (in billions of dollars)

Ethiopia 3.70
Others 0.86
Nigeria 0.33
Tanzania 0.26
Mozambique 0.17
Angola 0.27

Total = 5.59

Cuba and Latin America

Following the Berlin crisis in the second phase of the Cold War, Moscow capitalized on the revolution in Cuba led by Fidel Castro. On September 2, 1962, the USSR announced its intention of stepping up its military aid to Cuba. A few weeks later, peace was in danger of being shattered. On October 14, 1962, Washington had evidence of the installation on the island of Soviet intermediate range rockets. Tension between the two capitals was at its peak. On October 27, a letter from Khrushchev to President Kennedy offered to withdraw the missiles from Cuba in exchange for the withdrawal of American rockets from Turkey. With the drama averted, the Soviets still proclaimed their authority in the region, although it was seen as America's back yard.

During the last few years, the strategic importance of Latin America in the Soviet scheme of things has grown. The victory of the Sandinistas in Nicaragua marked Moscow's latest success. Helped by the Cubans, the USSR is trying to organise revolutionary movements in Guatemala, Honduras and Costa Rica. Cuba is the pivotal point in this policy. Arms donated by Latin American sympathizers pass through the island. The effective Soviet military presence in the region has risen to 4,700 men. A brigade of 2,600 soldiers is stationed on the outskirts of Havana, where there are also thousands of civilian advisers.

Aid given to Fidel Castro by Moscow now amounts to an annual total of 3.5 million dollars, not counting the donation of arms amounting to 60,000 tonnes in both 1981 and 1982. Today, Cuba possesses considerable military force including two *Polnocny* amphibious craft that arrived recently to reinforce the Havana fleet.

Soviet aid to Grenada was also growing. To a fairly negligible quantity of arms was added rolling stock for public transport, the promise of a site for receiving satellite communications, and the construction of a port and an airport on the east coast.

The rapid build-up of military power in Grenada posed such a problem to the Americans that they decided to intervene. Moscow protested vigorously, but it was a far cry from the missile crisis in Cuba. This was playing for totally different stakes. Such a hitch in the game did not discourage the Soviet Union, which continues to foment fierce anti-American sentiment in the region. This intervention by the USSR in Latin America, using Cuban forces, has had positive results for the time being.

Southern Africa

Angola, an old possession of Portugal's, is the key to Soviet intervention in Southern Africa. To add weight to the arrival in power of the MPLA, Moscow did not hesitate to establish East German and, above all, Cuban forces in the country. Tens of thousands of Cubans are stationed there. 3,000 to 4,000 Soviet troops encircle them in neighbouring states.

Although about ten Soviet warships are based at Luanda, attacks by UNITA guerillas and periodic incursions from South Africa do not make the government's life easy. On the Indian Ocean side, Mozambique is also supported by the Eastern bloc. President Samora Machel does what he can to keep his country 'non-aligned'.

This part of Africa is not vital for Soviet security. However, it is important to remember that the West is particularly dependent on this area. Its rich resources yield much of the West's raw materials. Also, the progressive African nations are seen as ripe for the development of Soviet ideology. In the last analysis, what causes Moscow to intervene in this region is, quite simply, the desire to assert its influence to the detriment of the West and China, which also has an interest in Southern Africa, notably in Angola and Tanzania.

Ethiopia

Moscow has made Ethiopia the dominant state of the horn of Africa. General Mengitsu's regime is largely indebted

Below Soviet military advisers training Angolan armed forces. *Right* MiG-21S and MiG-23S on a Cuban military aerodrome.

Delivery of Soviet military equipment to Cuba

Associated equipment (vehicles, food, uniforms, radio stations, spare guns)

Military equipment

SOVIET MIGS IN CUBA

Mig—23S

Mig—21S

to the Soviet Union, which is why he unreservedly supports the policies and the activities of the USSR. Ethiopia has become a base for activities aimed at destabilizing Somalia, Djibouti and the Sudan.

The Middle East
The Soviets have always wanted to play the primary role in the signing of any peace treaties in the Middle East, which obviously involves supporting the pro-Soviet regimes in the area. They find their most important customers for military equipment in the Arab world.

The USSR recognised the PLO in 1981. At the same time, relations with Syria were formalised in a friendship and co-operation treaty signed in October 1981. However, the Syrians and the Palestinians were none too pleased at the lack of support from their allies at the time of the invasion of the Lebanon by Israel. But in spite of everything, Moscow re-established its position by stepping up the quantity and quality of arms, particularly in surface-to-air missiles. After their expulsion from Egypt in 1976, the Soviets are gradually clawing back their influence in the Middle East, though in one area they are ever-watchful of their interests: Iran.

Iran poses a threat and a problem to the USSR. As well as having extensive oil resources, Iran shares a common border with the Soviet Union and controls the vital gate-

way to the Persian Gulf: the Straits of Hormuz. Furthermore, the fundamentalist Islamic regime is virulently anti communist. What the Russians fear is that current Islamic fervour will spill over into the Soviet Islamic states. It is also an area alive with danger and dispute: not least the four-year-old war between Iran and Iraq. Moscow supplies weapons to both sides, but would obviously not wish to see Iran as the victor.

South Yemen also represents an area open to Soviet influence. Aid in the form of equipment and advisors is gradually building up, threatening – in Western eyes – control of the Straits of Bab-el-Mandeb and access to the Red Sea and the Suez Canal.

But it was the Soviet invasion of Afghanistan that did most to bring turmoil to the area. Not only did it harden the anti-communist stance of the Iranians it alerted the West to the danger of potential Soviet expansion into the countries around the Persian Gulf.

The USSR now has some 100,000 soldiers stationed in Afghanistan together with tanks, artillery and the whole apparatus of an army of occupation. The fear that exists in the countries bordering Afghanistan is: where will they move to next?

South-East Asia
Soviet activity in this region is hampered by the power and

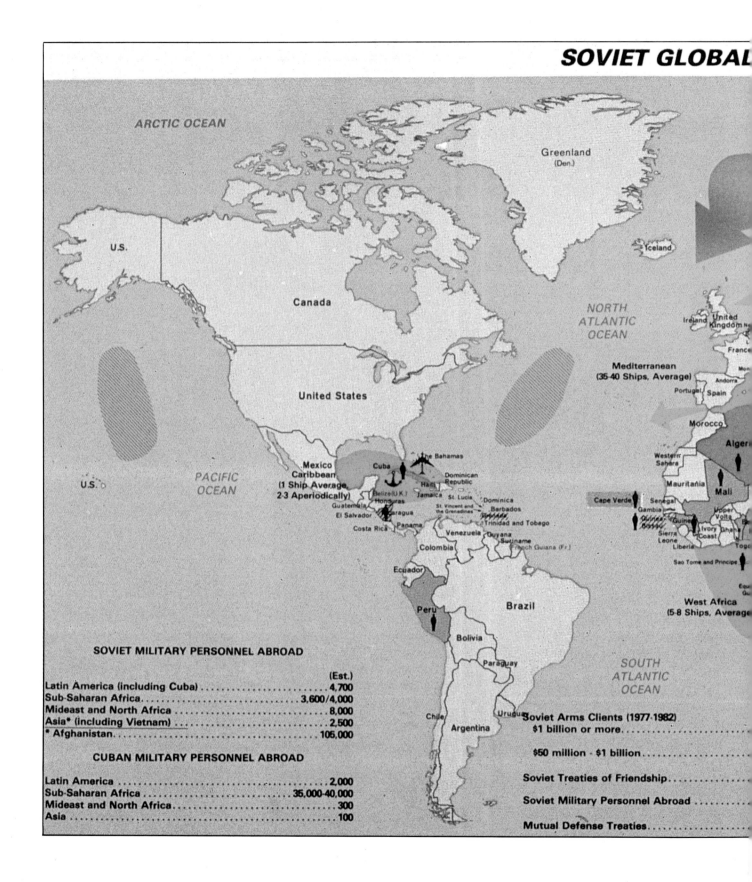

ARCTIC OCEAN

Greenland (Den.)

U.S.

Canada

Iceland

NORTH ATLANTIC OCEAN

Ireland United Kingdom

France

Mediterranean (35-40 Ships, Average)

Andorra

Portugal Spain

United States

Morocco

Western Sahara

Algeria

Mauritania

Mali

Mexico
Caribbean
(1 Ship Average,
2-3 Aperiodically)

Cuba

The Bahamas

Dominican Republic

Haiti

Jamaica

St. Lucia

Dominica

Barbados

Cape Verde

Senegal

Gambia

Guinea-Bissau

Guinea

Sierra Leone

Liberia

Ivory Coast

Ghana

Togo

Belize (U.K.)

Guatemala

Honduras

El Salvador

Nicaragua

Costa Rica

Panama

St. Vincent and the Grenadines

Grenada

Trinidad and Tobago

Venezuela

Guyana

Suriname

French Guiana (Fr.)

Sao Tome and Principe

Equatorial Guinea

Colombia

Ecuador

Peru

Brazil

West Africa
(5-8 Ships, Average

Bolivia

Paraguay

SOUTH ATLANTIC OCEAN

PACIFIC OCEAN

U.S.

Chile

Uruguay

Argentina

SOVIET MILITARY PERSONNEL ABROAD

	(Est.)
Latin America (including Cuba)	4,700
Sub-Saharan Africa	3,600/4,000
Mideast and North Africa	8,000
Asia* (including Vietnam)	2,500
* Afghanistan	105,000

CUBAN MILITARY PERSONNEL ABROAD

Latin America	2,000
Sub-Saharan Africa	35,000-40,000
Mideast and North Africa	300
Asia	100

Soviet Arms Clients (1977-1982)
$1 billion or more ......

$50 million - $1 billion ......

Soviet Treaties of Friendship ......

Soviet Military Personnel Abroad ......

Mutual Defense Treaties ......

WER PROJECTION

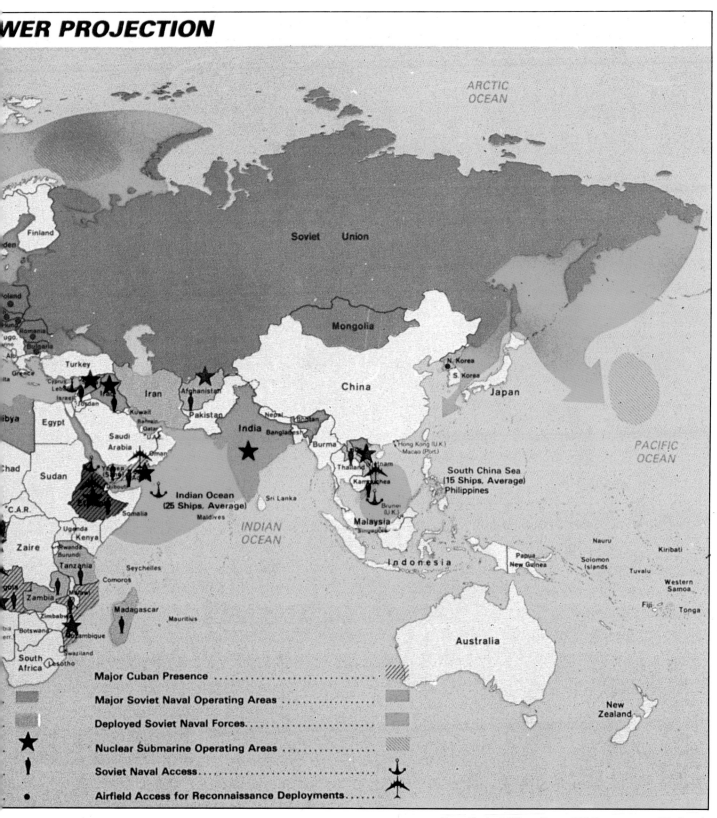

Legend:

- Major Cuban Presence
- Major Soviet Naval Operating Areas
- Deployed Soviet Naval Forces
- ★ Nuclear Submarine Operating Areas
- ↑ Soviet Naval Access
- • Airfield Access for Reconnaissance Deployments

From *Soviet Military Power* (US Department of Defense).

influence of China. Relations between the two largest communist states are cool to say the least. Though the Russians have made and continue to make political contacts with the Chinese, the Chinese have done little to improve relations with the Russians. And their coolness has been hardened by the build-up of Soviet forces on her borders. Today, the USSR has stationed on China's frontier 50 fully equipped divisions supported by 1,700 aircraft and about a third of the total number of SS-20s now at Moscow's disposal. The presence of these SS-20s has reinforced the traditional unease which the Chinese have always felt towards the Russians.

This is not to say that the Soviets have not tried to increase their influence in the area. Quite the contrary. Vietnam, Laos and Kampuchea have received the benefit of direct 'aid' from Moscow: aid now running to the tune of more than two thousand million dollars in military equipment alone, since 1979. There are also 2,500 'advisors' in the region. And in return for this 'aid' the Vietnamese have granted the Soviets a naval base at Cam Ran Bay – now an important Soviet intelligence and communications centre.

India represents, both historically and strategically, a prize for Soviet intrigue, infiltration and influence. India is one of the largest purchasers of arms in the Third World and offers rich pickings for the two superpowers. When Marshal Ustinov, the late Soviet Minister of Defence, visited the sub-continent in 1982, he did so with the express aim of selling arms to the Indians and to persuade the Indian government not to continue to buy arms from the West. In this he achieved a measure of success – in return for economic aid from Moscow. Today, the Soviet Union is India's largest trading partner and 80% of all India's military equipment is from the USSR.

Conclusions

This rapid tour around the world, although incomplete, shows in outline the Soviet Union's foreign policy. In all areas of the globe, the sale of arms is the chief means of acquiring political influence. The complementary nature of the military and economic aid granted by Moscow to the Third World is most potently expressed by the establishment of military bases in strategic areas. Lastly, Soviet support of all the communist regimes throughout the world reinforces the ideological credibility of the USSR and highlights 'socialism's march into the future'.

Despite the declared statements of the Soviet leaders, all is not well with the Soviet Union. The cost of furthering the 'onward march of socialism' is crippling. Official Soviet figures are modest: 3.4 per cent of the GNP. Western experts on the other hand estimate a more realistic 10-20 per cent of the Russian GNP. And such a burden for a country facing profound economic problems is deeply worrying for the new Soviet leadership under Gorbachov.

In an article published in the official organ *Krasnaya Zvezda*, dated December 9, 1982, Professor Major-General Gurov comments: '. . . demands on material provision for troops and naval forces have increased sharply . . . armies and navies are now equipped with the most complex systems of weapons and military hardware, which, furthermore, are virtually renewed every 10-12 years, which requires a highly developed and dynamic economy . . . there has been an increase in manpower costs and the cost of means of armed struggle and greater demands have been made on the moral-political qualities and general educational, technical and professional training both of workers engaged in military production and of the Armed Forces' personnel.'

Whether it is in the interests of the West for the Soviets to overcome these difficulties is a matter of debate.

Below Two *Katyusha* multiple rocket launchers seen in Chad in January 1977.

What makes Washington tick?

Above American marines and Guatemalan troops on manoeuvres. *Right* Commander and crewman of M1 *Abrams*.

The most basic characteristic of American military strategy is that it declares itself to be exclusively defensive. It is based on the nation's nuclear force and its capacity for technological innovation. In the last analysis, the United States is committed to protect its territories and to counteract what it sees as Soviet expansionism anywhere in the world. Washington's strategy is not linked to any specific ideology. According to the North Atlantic Treaty, it is founded on the safeguarding 'of the values that constitute the heritage of our civilization'.

Milestones in strategic policy

Since the end of World War 2, the Americans have had one enemy: the Soviet Union. Each important crisis (Berlin, Cuba, Afghanistan) is perceived by the United States as an act of aggression perpetrated by the Eastern bloc.

American strategy has seen many changes down the years, linked to the growing military power of the USSR. Nineteen-forty-five saw America in a position of supreme advantage. The Americans alone possessed nuclear weapons, enough to ensure them supremacy over the entire globe. This was, however, challenged in 1949 with the first Soviet atomic bomb test. To preserve their definite advantage over the Soviet Union, the USA developed even more sophisticated nuclear weaponry: thus the nuclear arms race war was born.

In order to avoid the proliferation of nuclear arms and the development of classical conflicts, from 1957 on the USA adopted a strategy known as 'massive retaliation'. Washington wanted to make sure of dissuading aggression.

Below Two American *AWACS* stationed on a military base west of Cairo.

by the Soviet Union anywhere in the world, especially in Europe.

In essence this policy threatened the USSR or its allies with massive nuclear retaliation if they launched a conventional attack on Western Europe. For its part, Europe renounced its former policy of resisting the USSR by conventional means.

However, this strategy had its limitations. Such a radical solution was not appropriate to the management of minor crises. Nuclear extremism has thus lost a large part of its previous credibility.

Flexible response

The Americans decided to rethink their principles by establishing a policy of 'flexible response'. This new concept was elaborated in the first years of the 1960s and its basis was a concept of the utmost flexibility in dealing with all possible forms of aggression. General Taylor, commander-in-chief of the US army during the Kennedy administration, put it this way: 'We must redefine our idea of large-scale war as being synonomous with the exchange of nuclear strikes between the United States and the Soviet Union. The term "limited warfare" will comprise all other forms of military operations.

'As to the question whether atomic weapons should be used in limited conflict the answer should be that one should first use conventional weapons while holding in reserve tactical nuclear weapons for the relatively rare cases where their use would further our national interest.'

This new American option necessitated a great variety of weapons which would allow for gradual escalation of the threat.

Pre-emptive strike

The new stage of American military strategy, 'counter-force strategy', alters the concept of flexible response.

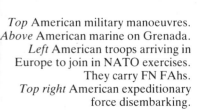

Top American military manoeuvres.
Above American marine on Grenada.
Left American troops arriving in Europe to join in NATO exercises. They carry FN FAhs.
Top right American expeditionary force disembarking.

This new orientation aims at sparing the centres of population as far as possible and directing the attack on the enemy's nuclear weapons sites. The Soviet Union has also adopted this strategy.

The deployment of SS-20 missiles on Soviet territory immediately provoked American and European reaction which was responsible for the arrival of the Pershing 2 and cruise missiles on European soil. The United States has to ensure an equal balance of nuclear force in the European theatre. America's policy in Europe comprises a classical offensive strategy towards the Soviet Union's military objectives which would destroy all likelihood of a prolonged attack by the USSR. This concept raises the possibility of a war of aggression launched by the Americans if faced with the imminence of a Soviet attack. And it is a prospect that is deeply worrying for all Europeans.

Europe in question

The fundamental question which exercises European minds has always been: given all the elaborate military strategies devised by Washington, are the Americans prepared to defend the old continent, blow by blow, against any Soviet offensive? It was because the United States had failed to formulate a clear policy on this matter that General de Gaulle decided to leave NATO in 1966 and create an independent nuclear force for France. Periodically, the Europeans demand guarantees, but it suits America to leave them in doubt. This kind of political blackmail condemns the European countries to dependence on their big brother in NATO.

The recent deployment of the first Euromissiles permits a partial solution to this problem. It means that in the event of a general conflict in Europe, the forces of the Atlantic Alliance, endowed by the US with tactical nuclear weapons, would establish the United States alongside Europe. But just where would this collaboration take place, and above all, is the US prepared to pay the heavy price of coming to Europe's aid?

The US position throughout the world

If it is a fact that America is determined to preserve its interests throughout the world, then it will intervene in every part of the globe where Soviet expansionism threatens to deprive it of any of its interests or risks disturbing the political or military balance.

Above Wading ashore: US Marines on a disembarcation exercise.

The structure of the American military presence abroad is quite different from the Soviet one. In the Eastern bloc, the Soviet Union is the only state which reserves the right to intervene anywhere in the world. In this way it has global supremacy over all the Warsaw Pact countries. The Soviet Union is helped in some places by the Cubans and the East Germans – in Angola, for example – but these nations play only the minor role assigned to them.

On the other hand, the West European countries have, since the passing of the colonial era, maintained their spheres of influence, their military bases and their political and economic affiliations. The United States can thus more or less officially, avoid intervening in conflicts where the shadow of Moscow looms. A case in point was Chad, where the Libyans, allies of the USSR, were fought on the ground by French troops.

Africa
The United States has never intervened much in Africa. It has left the Europeans to sort out as far as possible the problems caused by decolonization.

In certain areas, however, the USA has a number of troops on the ground to compensate for any imbalance which works against the interests of 'democracy'. The Americans obviously try to thwart Soviet hegemony as much as possible.

The Middle East
American policies in the Middle East have demonstrated Washington's desire to maintain the status quo as far as possible. The presence of US Marines in the recent crisis in Beirut, alongside French, Italian and British troops demonstrates the determination of the United States to see the Lebanon emerge as an autonomous state, free from Moscow's client state, Syria. And if Israel or its allies overreach themselves, Washington always has the power of withholding arms as the ultimate sanction to make sure its policies are pursued.

In the area of the Persian Gulf the United States has a prime role to play. It has declared its intention of keeping the Gulf open, by force if necessary, to ensure that supplies of oil reach its European allies. How quickly and efficiently the Americans would be able to field such force is open to debate, but certainly the intention is to have a 'rapid-deployment' force on call to intervene in any trouble spot in the area.

This force, in fact, is seen as a larger, global, commitment recently undertaken by the USA. The aim is to set up – at a moment's notice – a fighting force able to meet trouble anywhere in the world. These forces would be based on a logistic system of airfields and naval bases stretching across the world. Chief among them are the US bases on the Azores, Western Europe, Portugal, Morocco, northern Cyprus, Diego-Garcia, Somalia and Oman.

South-East Asia
The American presence in South-East Asia also relies on a network of bases which form a logistic chain for the smooth running of an expansionist operation directed against the territories of the USSR. The Americans have also established themselves in like manner in the Philippines, Korea, Japan and South Korea.

Latin America
Its proximity to US territory means that the Americans have constantly to monitor the volatile political situation in Latin America.

The recent intervention in Grenada shows that Washington will never let the debacle of Cuba happen again. The fact that the Cubans and the Soviets conceived the idea of building a 3,000 m runway provoked the American reaction. A similar infrastructure served as a stopping off place for transport planes for Cuban troops bound for Africa and received fighter and reconnaissance aircraft from the Soviet Union.

Firmer policy
Since the arrival of Ronald Reagan at the White House, the United States seems to be adopted a less flexible line towards the Soviet Union. The Secretary of State of Defense, Caspar Weinberger, has reaffirmed American determination to combat the Soviet threat throughout the world.

Consistently the Reagan administration has accused the Soviet Union of being the main instigator of global instability: in the Middle East, in Latin America, Southern Africa, the Far East and in America's own backyard, Mexico. And when in March 1983 the US President characterized the Soviets as an 'evil empire' and its regime as a 'bizarre chapter' destined for the 'dustheap of history' it seemed as if the cold war had returned with a vengeance.

CHEMICAL AND BIOLOGICAL WARFARE

Hell on earth

Understandably, the deployment of American missiles in Western Europe has made Europeans particularly aware of the dangers of a general nuclear confrontation. Yet this vision of the apocalypse has pushed into the background an equally terrifying threat to peace: the vast stock-piles of chemical and biological weapons lying dormant on European soil. Is it conceivable that the two super-powers would use these hideous weapons of destruction? One thing is plain: little is being done to control their manufacture and deployment in Europe today . . .

The shape of things to come? US troops await a gas attack wearing their NBC (nuclear, biological and chemical) equipment. *Inset* A Soviet gas mask, used in Afghanistan, goes on show in the USA.

The idea of a biological or chemical attack in whatever theatre of war frightens us all. We all know that deployment of these so-called 'special' weapons on a grand scale would have consequences impossible to calculate. Everybody agrees that biological and chemicals weapons are abominable: the idea of having to face an attack by gas or microbes is inconceivable. Yet in spite of this, both East and West hold enormous stocks of these weapons which could destroy the planet several thousand times over.

Chemical weapons are defined by the United Nations as: 'substances, whether gaseous, liquid or solid, which could be used because of their direct toxic effect against people, animals and plants', and bacterial agents of war are defined as 'living organisms, whatever their nature, or infectious substances derived from these organisms, intended to provoke death or disease in people, animals or plants, the effects of which are a function of their ability to multiply in the person, animal or plant under attack'.

Lethal, incapacitating and neutralising agents
This fairly vague definition has been further refined by the World Health Organisation (WHO), into a more realistic and detailed classification. Toxic, chemical or biological agents can be grouped into three main categories: lethal, incapacitating or neutralising agents.

Lethal agents
'They are invented to cause death as soon as people are exposed to them in concentrations easily made available in military operations.'

Incapacitating agents
'Destined to provoke illness or mental or physical incapacity for a temporary period whose duration far exceeds the period of exposure.'

Neutralising agents
'They are also termed "incapacitating agents of short duration". They rapidly provoke incapacity which lasts about as long as the period of exposure.'

This three-fold classification is basic. Too often governments have clouded the issue of chemical and biological weapons by maintaining that they are not manufacturing chemicals of a lethal nature, but the less obnoxious sounding 'incapacitating agents', or harmless 'neutralising agents'. The idea that a gas can be used that does not kill or maim but merely 'immobilizes' for a short time is obviously appealing. And the old dream of being able to win wars or control whole populations without firing a shot still exercizes the minds of strategists the world over. The truth of what these chemical and biological agents really do, however, is rather different.

Agents of biological warfare
Over and above the first World Health Organization classification, each principal agent in each category and their specific effects can be further defined.

First is the subject of biological warfare. The agent in this case is a micro-organism (bacterium or virus). This organism must possess certain specially defined qualities to belong to this category. It must be as contagious as possible, leave its victims without any immunity, possess a very short incubation period and offer as little danger as possible to the user in case he is affected too.

Having fulfilled these criteria, such agents fall into four groups: 'viral infections', 'rickets infections', 'bacterial infections' and 'fungus infections'.

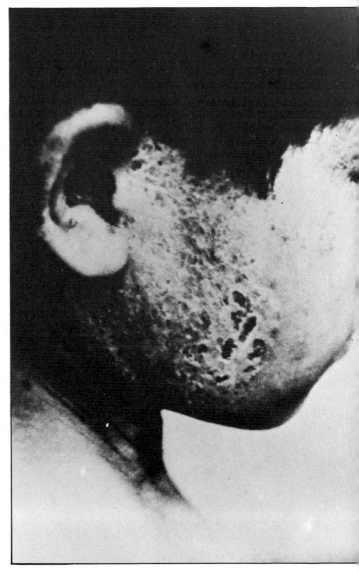

Above A photograph that supports – according to the USA – their claim that the Russians have used chemical weapons in Afghanistan. It shows the effects of mustard gas or of a deadly neurotoxic on the skin of an Afghan child.

Viral infections
Viruses are the smallest living organic substances in the world. Only vaccination can combat them, if carried out in time. In the case of massive contamination, it is doubtful if the health services of the country attacked would be able to combat the ravages caused by the virus. Among these micro-organisms are smallpox, yellow fever and certain very virulent varieties of 'flu.

Rickets infections
These are micro-organisms similar to bacteria. Their dissemination by aerosol would wreak havoc very easily since the contaminated populations would not possess vaccines and antibiotics in sufficient quantities. Among the best known are typhus – judged to be too easy to cure to fit the first requirement of this category – purple fever of the Rocheuses mountains and Queensland fever, which is more incapacitating than deadly.

Bacterial infections
These simple unicellular structures are part of the vegetable kingdom, and are less formidable than viruses on the whole. If selected with care, however, they can cause a lot

of damage. Their principal characteristics are very well known. In the past they caused plagues: the most impressive being pulmonary plague, which only streptomycine can attempt to cure. Easily preserved thanks to lyophilization this bacterium can cause an incontrollable 'reverse action' which limits its use. Another formidable bacterium is anthrax. This can act by contact, by ingestion and by inhalation. If antibiotics are not given immediately, death is almost certain for everyone attacked. The use made of anthrax by the British on the island of Gruinard, in Scotland, in 1942 illustrates the virulence of this biological agent. Ground contaminated by anthrax will always be unsafe; and the island is, even today, completely unapproachable.

Two other pathogenic bacteria are equally dangerous: those resulting in brucellosis and typhoid fever.

Fungal infections
These are caused by mushrooms, toadstools and funguses. The most famous, desert fever, is transmitted by *Coccidiodes immitis*. Dispersed in the form of aerosols, after a fortnight's incubation it produces a state not unlike 'flu. It is more incapacitating than deadly.

Agents of chemical warfare
This category comprises all forms of gas which have been used in battle. These weapons would be used to overcome a badly trained and poorly equipped enemy. For any potential user there are about a hundred of these chemical compounds at their disposal. They are grouped in accordance with their mode of action.

Above A Soviet plane in Afghanistan of the type which the Americans say have been used to release toxic chemicals over the countryside. *Below left* The reality: a US paratrooper with Airborne 101st AA flashes, giving instruction on how to use NBC equipment.

Lethal agents
These gases are meant to kill. They are of three kinds. The first comprises asphyxiants and gases that cause blistering. The asphyxiants attack the respiratory tracts – in this category are chlorine and phosgene. Blistering gases cause cruel burns on contaminated skin. In a few days the infection spreads. For those directly exposed, death invariably follows after a period of between a few days to a few weeks. The best known blistering agent is mustard gas, a gas with a pungent smell, first used in 1917.

The second group of lethal gases is even more horrible. These are the haemotoxins and nerve gases. The former were used by the Germans in the gas chambers of World War 2. The contaminated person loses conciousness soon

after inhaling the gas. A few seconds later he dies through respiratory failure. The principal gases of this type are cynanide acid and cyanogen chloride.

Nerve gases are by far the most formidable. Their effects are well known in all the armies in the world: the nose begins to run, troubled vision follows, breathing becomes more and more difficult and the contaminated person soon begins to vomit and defecate. Headaches are quickly followed by mental disturbance. The next stage is coma, then convulsions and finally death occurs when breathing is arrested.

Neurotoxic gas is colourless and odourless and quickly attacks the central nervous system. Two substances can serve as an antidote to some extent: atropine and oxime. These agents can be type 'G' (tabun, sarin, soman) or type 'V' (VE, VM, VX).

The last group of lethal agents is made up of toxins. The manufacture and stock-piling of these substances is officially forbidden. Even so, they are grouped into three categories: phytotoxins, zootoxins and microbe toxins.

Phytotoxins, of vegetable origin, are formidable poisons, among which are strychnine and curare. These two deadly substances work through progressive paralysis of the striated muscles leading rapidly to death through respiratory failure.

Zootoxins are derived from animal venom (for example, snakes and fish).

Microbe toxins are produced by micro-organisms. The most severe can cause botulism. The WHO has drawn up a scenario which envisages the action of the botulism toxin on a population of 50,000. The deadly substance could be introduced through the water supply. 250 grammes would be enough. 'Introducing the toxin would take six hours (from midnight to 6 am), ending with the appearance of the

Left Two US soldiers kitted out in full NBC uniforms man a guided missile somewhere in Europe. *Below* Chemical warfare knows no boundaries: decontamination equipment being tested in neutral Switzerland.

first symptoms. The rate of initial concentration, from entry into the water supply, is 0.05 mg per litre.

'At 5.30 pm, 10% of the inhabitants would have absorbed a lethal dose eight hours previously. If countermeasures were taken at that time, 30,000 people would have already received the lethal dose. If the danger had been identified an hour earlier, at 4.30 pm, so that the symptoms would have shown up in 1,200 people, the number of those having already taken a lethal dose would fall to about 28,000'.

Incapacitating agents
These agents have a less severe effect than the ones described previously. For some military people, this category of gas represents the 'best option'. Soldiers would not be killed on the battlefield any more. They would be taken prisoner, suffering from a 'passing indisposition'. These agents are, however, far from being harmless. And their threat is of two types: physical and psychological. The aim of the first is to diminish the muscular activity of those affected. This is achieved characteristically by inducing nausea and diarrhoea. Known as 'ES' *(enterotoxins staphylococci)* the manufacture and stock-piling of these substances is prohibited by international convention.

Psychological incapacitants act on the brain, provoking temporary mental aberrations. The best known is LSD. The principal drawback of this special type of weapon is that it provokes unforeseen and uncontrollable reactions in its victim. What, for example, would happen to those who possessed tactical nuclear weapons . . .?

Neutralising agents
According to the WHO, neutralising agents are 'chemical agents, which, used in effective operational concentrations, are capable of causing temporary disability whose length would hardly exceed the period of exposure'. They are different from incapacitants in that the effects are immediate and the contamination less persistent. The principal agents in this category are sneezing powders (which irritate the respiratory tracts) and tear gases (which irritate the eyes).

Phytotoxic agents
These products are reserved for the destruction of plants. The main ones are herbicides which destroy vegetation or sterilising agents which interfere with the growth of vegetables. The effects of these agents is so radical that the ground remains barren for many years, obliging the population to move to avoid dying of hunger.

Means of attack
Whether they are chemical or biological, the efficacy of these special weapons is measured by how effectively they are employed and the way in which they are spread. There are many methods of use.

Chemical attack
Chemical attack can take place on the ground or from the air. On the ground, contaminated ammunition can be fired by mortars, cannons, howitzers, rockets or missiles. Light weapons can be used to fire 'short-life agents', that is, those volatile enough to contaminate an area in only a few minutes. In contrast, heavy weapons can fire 'long-lasting agents' forbidding access to the zone without protection for several hours or days. Chemical raids from the air are carried out by bombs, filled with contaminated agents, or by spraying.

Biological attack

There are three methods of biological contamination. The first is effected by the use of explosives. Aersols can also be used. They eject under pressure a substance containing selected micro-organisms in suspension. The third method involves spraying contaminated liquid in a jet of air at great speed. All three techniques are very sophisticated, though it is always possible, even though experts might think it fairly remote, that a single man – an enemy agent, for example – might poison a water supply or a ventilation system on this own.

The effect of these biological weapons would be considerable. The Group for Research and Information on Peace estimate that a one megatonne nuclear bomb would affect 300 square kilometres. Fifteen tonnes of neurotoxic agents would affect 60 square kilometres and ten tonnes of biological agents would contaminate almost 100,000 square kilometres.

International reaction

The use of gas during World War 1 created a pronounced public reaction. A document was signed in 1925 in Geneva prohibiting the use in war of toxic asphyxiating gases and other similar gases, and the use of biological weapons (according to the old categories of special chemical and biological weapons). 'We the undersigned, in the name of our respective governments, believing that the use in times of war of asphyxiating, toxic and other similar gases, also all liquids, substances or processes of a similar nature, have been rightly condemned by the public opinion of the civilized world . . . declare that the powers here represented, in so far as they are not already party to treaties prohibiting their use, recognise this prohibition, accept that it must be extended to biological warfare and agree to consider themselves bound by the terms of this declaration.' This text was signed on June 17 by 26 countries.

This international reaction, which placed special chemical and biological weapons outside the law, had been preceded by other, less important treaties; the Washington Pact of February 6, 1922, for example.

On December 16, 1969, a series of resolutions on the subject of chemical and biological weapons was adopted by the General Assembly of the United Nations. On this occasion, the Secretary General 'took note of the convention's plan for the prohibition of the invention, manufacturing and stockpiling of chemical and bacteriological (chemical) weapons and of the destruction of existing stocks, presented to the Assembly by delegations from Hungary, Bulgaria, Mongolia, Poland, the Soviet Socialist Republic of Belorussia, the Socialist Republic of the Ukraine, of Romania, Czechoslovakia and the USSR . . .'

This time, it was the Eastern bloc that proposed the destruction of existing stocks, and the United States that did not immediately ratify the Geneva protocol. And it was not until April 10, 1975, in fact, that the Americans agreed – but not without reservation – to accept the text of 1925. Other nations also hesitated to commit themselves, reserving some sort of 'right of reply' in time of war. For example, France wanted to include in the protocol some new elements, notably: 'the said protocol will cease to exercise any obligation on the government of the French Republic in respect of any enemy whose forces or whose allies no longer respect the prohibitions which constitute the object of this protocol.'

Above While other European nations have procrastinated, the Swiss have built nuclear shelters for its citizens. Here a Swiss civilian emerges from his shelter wearing NBC gear.

The situation on the ground

Though international negotiations aimed at outlawing the use of these 'special weapons' have been going on since 1925, there is evidence to suggest that their use has been widespread on battlefields throughout the world throughout this century. Most of the evidence is conclusive while some remains circumstantial.

The Stockholm International Peace Research Institute (SIPRI) has researched the use (proven or non-proven) of toxic gases, chemical herbicides or pathogenic micro-organisms in all parts of the world since the end of World War 1.

Use of toxic gases and toxins

— PROVEN:
    1925: Spain against Morocco
    1934: USSR against China
    1935: Italy against Ethiopia
    1937: Japan against China
    World War 2: Germany in the extermination camps
— UNPROVEN:
    1951: United States against North Korea
    1957: France against Algerian insurgents
    1961: United States against Vietnam
    1965: Iraq against The Kurds
    1979: USSR against Afghanistan
    1980: Ethiopia against secession in Eritrea
    1982: Israel against The PLO

Use of chemical herbicides
— PROVEN:
    1950: Britain against Malaysian insurgents
    1959: France against Algerian insurgents
    1961: United States against Vietnam
    1968: Portugal against Angola and Mozambique
— UNPROVEN:
    1981: Ethiopia against Eritrea

Use of biological agents
— PROVEN:
    1940: Japan against China
— UNPROVEN:
    1942: Polish and Soviet resistance against the Germans
    1951: United States in Korea

Accidents
The invention, experimentation, stockpiling and the manufacture of these products sometimes leads to spectacular accidents. The British experience on the island of Gruinard in 1942 has already been mentioned. To this may be added the destruction in 1943 of an allied vessel carrying mustard gas off Bari. One thousand Italians were contaminated and perished. More recently, in 1968 a defective container in the United States leaked some incapacitating gas, causing the death of more than 6,000 sheep. American sources also claim that an epidemic of anthrax broke out in an area of Sverdkovsk in 1979, probably as a result of an explosion that took place in a factory specialising in the manufacture of biological weapons.

The situation today
In spite of protocols binding many countries, the world has witnessed many full-scale tests and acts of aggression involving the use of chemical and biological weapons.

In his book *The Third World War* General Sir John Hackett traces the hypothetical scenario of the development of World War 3. He considers the possibility of a chemical attack at the outset of hostilities. 'From the outset the assailant (the Warsaw Pact) could take the initiative with the use of chemical and nuclear weapons.

'It is obvious that the biological option would not be used, but the West has to conduct operations which takes into account the possibility of having to counter an attack employing the two other means (chemical and nuclear). Its effectiveness is thus lessened – perhaps by 50% by the necessity of having to provide protection against chemical and nuclear attack.' The option open to the British is quite clear: no recourse to biological weapons, but a massive use of chemical compounds.

The thesis of the SIPRI is even more alarming: 'The menace to national security which has slowed down progress on the control of chemical and biological warfare . . . has become more evident, and the type of response that governments can offer has become more and more limited. Of course, the possibility of negotiated disarmament in this field is always open at Geneva, but unless the declaration of intent by certain world leaders is not translated into action soon, this possibility will disappear. In the meantime, the desire to pursue unilaterally all-out military preparation for chemical and biological warfare could soon lead irreversibly to a new and preposterous arms race.'

Ricardo Frailé, Secretary General of the Centre for Study and Research on Disarmament is of the opinion that

Above Life goes on deep underground in an NBC shelter. *Right* France's answer to the threat of chemical and biological attack.

'If nations continue to accumulate more and more toxic agents, the whole idea of chemical and biological disarmament will be discredited. In spite of juridical prohibitions, these types of armaments are being gradually and imperceptibly rehabilitated.'

East-West rivalry
The frightening rivalry between East and West is at the centre of this terrifying escalation. In 1982, the United States accused the Soviet Union of having used chemical weapons in Afghanistan. Secretary for Defense Alexander Haig stated that 'since 1979, the Soviet forces in Afghanistan have used all kinds of lethal and non-lethal chemical agents against the Mudjahidin resistance forces and Afghan villages . . . This information is confirmed by proof of symptoms reported that are evidence of the use of neurotoxics, phosgene gas and certain other incapacitants and irritants.'

The Soviets sent their reply to these accusations to the United Nations Secretary General on May 20 of the same year: 'The report is based on unconfirmed hearsay, on interviews with those pretending to be witnesses and on other material of doubtful origin.'

While the politicians bicker, the manufacture and deployment of these awesome weapons is escalating. In 1982 the US government began the general re-armament in chemical and biological weapons. President Reagan was not long in confirming this in language typical of the cold war warrior: 'The production of lethal binary chemical weapons is essential for the national interest.'

France, possessing the biggest arsenal of these weapons after the USA and the USSR, has been promoting the idea that they represent as effective a deterrent to war as *nuclear* weapons. But though the French may possess the largest stocks of chemical and biological weapons in Europe, it is meagre when compared to that at the disposal of the USSR: estimated by a recent British Minister of Defence to be some 300,000 tonnes.

Is there any protection?

To counter the use of chemical and biological weapons on the battlefield the armies of NATO and the Warsaw Pact have been issued with a variety of protective clothing.

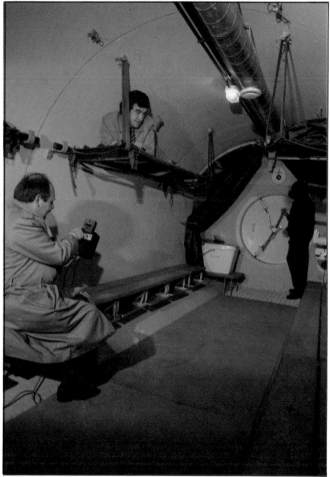

Left If the USA should ever become the target of a chemical attack this is how some of its citizens would meet it. *Above* Inside a nuclear shelter, French style.

How effective such clothing is, is open to doubt. But research under simulated battlefield conditions seems to suggest that it does offer a measure of protection against certain chemicals for a short time.

Typical of this clothing is the '66' uniform worn by the French army, claimed to offer protection against toxic agents for about six hours. It consists of a set of overalls; a cagoule with a protective hood – which can be used as a mask or NAP ('normal apparatus of protection'); a pair of rubber boots; two pairs of rubber gloves together with a pair of cotton gloves and a set of brush-cotton underpants.

The overalls are a single garment. The cagoule and its hood covers the head, shoulders and the opening behind the overalls. The NAP – more commonly known as a gas mask – is the most important part of this equipment. It must protect the respiratory tract, the eyes and the face against nuclear, chemical and biological (NCB) agents. It is made up of a moulded rubber face covering; a helmet consisting of a set of moulded rubber adjustable straps; two eye-pieces fitted with anti-vapour film; a case containing, and protecting the maintenance valve and a cartridge filter.

The cartridge is the essential element of the NAP. It is made up of two parts, a paper anti-aerosol filter and an anti-vapour filter containing a bed of charcoal impregnated with a neutralising substance. It offers effective protection against poisons for up to five days.

Wearing this elaborate and cumbersome equipment obviously inhibits the fighting effectiveness of the soldier at the front. But at least he is afforded some measure of protection. If a general war were to break out in Europe and civilians were exposed to the effects of chemical agents there is little protection available for them. A simple gas mask of the kind favoured by most governments would offer no protection against a neurotoxic attack. With little help most civilians would be thrown back on their own resources.

Faced with this fate most would suffer a slow, painful and lingering death. And though the spectre of biological warfare seems now to have faded, it is because of the technical difficulties in controlling the effects of micro-organisms – rather than any moral or humane scruples. Indeed the abandonment of biological agents as weapons of war has accelerated the deployment of chemical agents. In the event of a large scale conflict involving the super-powers, 'special weapons' of a chemical kind would almost certainly be used. It is, however, impossible to predict the extent to which they would be employed – or the amount of suffering they would cause.

CHEMICAL AGENTS WHICH MAY BE USED IN FUTURE WARFARE

Name	Type	Effect
Tabun (GA) Sarin (GB) Soman (GD) VX	Nerve Agents In gas or liquid form.	Breathing difficulty, runny nose blurred vision, nausea, sweating, vomiting, giddy, muscular spasms, paralysis, death.
Distilled Mustard or Nitrogen Mustard	Blister Agents In gas or liquid form.	Eye and skin irritation. Blisters, external (and internal if inhaled or swallowed) Bronchopneumonic Effects, following initial irritation may be delayed up to 48 hours! Can prove fatal immediately or after years of illness.
Phosgene	Choking Agent Gas.	Damages lungs. Victim coughs and drowns in his own fluid.
CN DM CS BZ	Incapacitating Agents Gases.	Irritates eyes and skin. Breathing difficulty. Nausea and vomiting. For BZ, flushed skin, irregular heartbeat, high pulse-rates, hallucinations, maniacal behaviour.
Botulin (X & A) Ricin Saxitoxin (TZ) Entero-toxin (B) Tetrodotoxin	Toxin Agents In powder or liquid forms.	Blurred vision, tingling limbs, headaches, numbness, fatigue, cramps, breathing difficulty, dizziness, vomiting, paralysis, death.
LSD and other mind affecting drugs	Psycho Agents In gas, liquid, or powder.	High pulse rate, flushed skin, hallucinations, incapacity to think clearly, open to suggestion. Stupors. Unconsciousness?

PERSONAL
FIRE
ARMS

The infantryman's weapons

In the first hours of a nuclear war, individual firearms will obviously be useless, since their potential for destruction is dwarfed by the might of megatons. But sooner or later, war becomes conquest and a man will find himself face to face with his enemy – another man. And it is then that the best weapon will win through.

Hand guns have always exercised a fascination for men. The attraction of cold metal and the power of killing from a controlled distance have played a very important part in this fascination.

Today, the diverse vicissitudes of the arms race between the superpowers has concealed this fact somewhat. When we speak of 'weapons', we immediately think of heavy weapons: bombers, missiles, tanks, etc. – all the panoply which make a nation into a warlike power. The entry of nuclear weapons into this deadly game has deepened the divide. In films such as *The Day After*, the sight of a nuclear bomb exploding over a city makes the use of a revolver or a machine-gun for self-defence seem derisory.

And yet, who knows what form a future war will take? Who can say that in a month, a year or several years, enemy armies will not confront each other with hand guns face to face? And even if the menace of a nuclear conflict does exist, it is luckily only a hypothesis at the present time. It is a different matter with individual firearms. They are in use in all the hot spots of the world. Terrorists are armed with them and they help resistance movements and wars of independence to achieve their ends. No conflict takes place without the use of individual firearms.

Faced with such a reality, it is useful to know the history, development and the particular qualities of each of these weapons: revolvers, rifles, sub-machine guns, machine guns and anti-tank weapons. The story started long ago when men carried off their trophies at the point of their bayonets. These now belong in glass cases in museums, but their descendants are the subject of endless discussion in the armed forces of both superpower camps.

Revolvers and pistols

France was the first European country to use the revolver as a regular weapon. This was the Lefaucheux Marine model at the end of the 1850s At this time the revolver was loaded by introducing in turn powder and a ball in each chamber of the barrel, and placing a fuse (detonator) on each nipple. Although its performance was comparable with that of modern revolvers, these weapons had an annoying disadvantage: they took too long to reload. The area of development was thus in loading by the breech using complete cartridges.

Three prestigious names occur in the history of the revolver. First, there is Leonardo da Vinci. He had explained in 1490 the technique of the 'wheel-lock' pistol in which the powder is set alight by the friction of a grooved disc on a stone.

The second name is even more famous in this field – that of Colonel Samuel Colt. Born in Harford, Connecticut, Colt acquired patents in the United States and England. When Colt's various patents expired, a great step forward was taken, thanks to Smith and Wesson and their cylinder which could be loaded from the breech with a modern type of cartridge. From a mechanical standpoint, the modern revolver reached its peak at the beginning of the twentieth century and its concept has hardly changed since. It was also at this time that a new type of hand gun made its appearance: the semi-automatic pistol.

As a general rule, the revolver contains six cartridges. One of its advantages is that is comfortable to use. It is less messy than its competitor, can be carried safely fully loaded and is ready to fire immediately, without the necessary of having to operate a safety catch or anything else to slow matters down.

Top left A Sudanese paratrooper learns how to handle an American *M-16*. *Centre left* An American soldier trains Egyptian soldiers to fire an AK-47 assault rifle. *Bottom left* An American soldier equipped with a *LAW* recoilless anti-tank weapon. *Above* The *IAI B-300* anti-tank weapon. *Above right* The PA-50 pistol used in the French army.

The automatic pistol contains eight cartridges and sometimes even more. It is more accurate than the revolver and easier to conceal. Nevertheless it has certain important disadvantages: it is more complicated, more prone to lock and often slower to put into action – due to the danger of leaving a cartridge in the chamber. Despite these disadvantages, however, it is used in most of the world's armies.

The difference between the revolver and the semi-automatic pistol became apparent during World War 1. Opinion was divided between the devotees of the 'old' system – the revolver – and those who preferred weapons like the Colt 1911. This battle between the two systems still continues among the experts. And in the military field, the future of the pistol is no longer assured. Except for secret missions, the sub-machine gun or the assault rifle are greatly preferred to the hand-gun, particularly with troops in the field.

Bergmann, Luger and others . . .

Among the best known and most common French revolver is the *Lebel* which entered service in 1892 and was used until World War 2. Named after Colonel Lebel, a weapons expert, it weighs 0.79 kg and has an 8 mm calibre.

In terms of semi-automatic pistols, France has produced the *Mab model B*, made at the weapons factory in Bayonne. First introduced in 1921, this pistol has proved to be very successful, both in France and abroad. There are many versions, including a 9 mm calibre and 7.65 mm calibre.

Germany and Britain have been important producers of hand-guns. The semi-automatic was dominant in Germany. The oldest is the *Bergmann*, which is very rare today, but which existed in several versions. There is also the *Walther P 8*, an excellent weapon adopted as standard issue by the German army in World War 2. It is a 9 mm, like the *Parabellum P 08*, or 'Luger'. The latter, although

performing less well, has earned itself a solid reputation throughout the world. The Swiss army was the first to use it.

The English, on the other hand, have shown a preference for revolvers. Following each other closely in Britain were the *Webley and Scott Mark I* and *Mark IV*, the *Webley and Scott Mark VI*, made in huge quantities, the *Webley-Fosbery*, which had only a small success and lastly the .38 calibre *Enfield No 2 Mark I*, fired by a simple pressure on the trigger.

Since 1930, the Soviet Union has favoured a pistol inspired by the Americans *Colt* and *Browning*, called the *Tula-Tokarev*. This very effective weapon has one drawback: although its ammunition is very powerful, 1600 f/p/s, it is not very accurate. It is also manufactured by other Warsaw Pact countries.

The United States is without question the nation with the highest reputation in the field of semi-automatic pistols. The first in the series was the *Colt*, a weapon used on a grand scale by the US army during World War 1. There is no doubt that it is the most reliable weapon of its type ever invented, and is still widely used today.

American designed, but not used in the US Army is the *Browning*. This 9 mm calibre weapon took the name of its inventor, John Browning. It is regulation issue in many countries. Even the British, who were faithful to the revolver for many years, have adopted it.

Rifles

The rifle has played a dominant role in every army, even before the twentieth century. But it was World War 1 that established the rifle as the infantryman's specialist weapon. The British in particular obtained remarkable results with the *Lee Enfield .303* magazine-loaded rifle. In the opening months of the war the Germans were astonished by its speed and precision.

In 1939, at the outbreak of World War 2, both the Germans and the Allies were equipped with rifles of a similar type with similar capabilities.

On the German side was the *Kar 98 K*, a shortened version of the 1898 model; the British were still equipped with the *Lee Enfield* and the French with the famous *Mas 1936*. The latter is a magazine rifle based on the German Mauser, but whose movable breech is designed to lock in the upper part of the weapon, behind the magazine. A folding version of this weapon was used in Indo-China in the 1950s, particularly by the paratroopers of the French Foreign Legion. The *Mas 1949* which succeeded it, is no longer in service.

The US army is the only one to be equipped throughout

with a semi-automatic rifle. This is the *Garand M1 30*, which, in its different forms, is the most widespread of all those manufactured in the United States. Its total production has already passed the seven million mark. Since the traditional rifle with a long range no longer seemed adequate, it became necessary to find an intermediate weapon.

This piece of equipment, a sort of improved sub-machine gun, was named an assault rifle. The Germans were the first to experiment with this kind of weapon with their *MP 43*, followed by the *MP 44*. Introduced into service during World War 2, this model consequently served as the basis for a great number of assault rifles, in particular the Soviet army's *Kalashnikov AK 47*. Introduced in 1951, the *Kalashnikov* had originally a wooden butt, later changed to a folding metal butt system – particularly favoured by airborne troops for its compactness.

The folding butt also makes the weapon easier to conceal – a fact that has led to the *Kalashnikov* becoming popular with terrorists and guerrillas, who also favour it for its easy handling.

The US army also has its *Kalashnikov*: the *Colt Armalite M16-M16A1*. The British have the *Sterling Armalite AR-18*.

Main assault rifles

The Armalite has been the most successful weapon in the United States after the *M1 A1*. Production of the prototype, the *AR 10*, began in 1955 and was followed by the *AR 15 M 16*, more commonly known as the *M 16*. Adopted by the American army in Vietnam, this rifle is now standard issue for US troops, except those assigned to NATO. It has also found favour with armies of the Far East because of its ease of handling and lightness.

The *EM2* was rejected by Britain, despite its good reputation, in favour of the 7.62 mm, lighter *Individual Weapon*, which replaced all the British rifles and sub-machine guns. The Belgians had set the scene in this category of lighter and smaller weapons with the FN *Fal*. This light automatic rifle has proved to be very successful in all its different versions.

Another weapon in general use today is the 5.56 mm calibre *FA MAS*, adopted as a regulation rifle by the French army at the end of the 1970s. Its original profile, with a very long butt has given it the name of *Bugle*. This new generation of weapons also includes an Israeli rifle called the *Gallil*, adopted by the defence forces in 1972. It is also made in Sweden under the name of *FFV 890 C*.

On the Soviet side, the famous *AK 47* has been replaced by a lightened, mass-produced version of the original AK called the *AKM*. The AK74 is the most common assault rifle in the world – a splendid success for the designer, Michael Kalashnikov.

Sub-machine guns

Sub-machine guns are automatic weapons which use pistol cartridges. Thanks to their lightness, they can be fired either from the shoulder or from the hip. The first to use them were the Italians with their *Villar Perosa*. A few years later, in 1918, the first examples of the German *MP 18*, equally well known under the name of *Bergmann*, made their appearance. Production reached 35,000 in a few months. The *Bergmann* served as the prototype for most of the weapons of this type manufactured afterwards.

In France, American Colonel Thompson was the first to foresee the sub-machine gun's possibilities during World

The popular, internationally favoured, *Kalashnikov* rifle: *Far left* Angola; *above* and *inset* South America.

War 1. Unfortunately, the first version did not appear until after the 1914-18 war. It was nonetheless a great success with IRA terrorists and with gangsters during prohibition in the United States in the 1920s and '30s. It was not until the beginning of World War 2, however, that the Thompson or 'Tommy gun' really came into its own as a military weapon.

The British Sten gun was another success story. Manufactured in millions, there has been a series of models which have progressively simplified its action.

Prohibited by the terms of the Treaty of Versailles of introducing a new and up-to-date sub-machine gun, the Germans continued, officially, to supply their army with antiquated *Bergmanns*, while developing and manufacturing the *Steyr-Solothurn* sub-machine gun in Switzerland from 1922 onwards under cover of a Swiss company. This programme resulted in the *MP 38* introduced into the German army in 1938. It was a very modern weapon, made entirely of metal and provided with a folding butt. When war broke out in 1939 it was soon to prove its worth and gained an enviable reputation throughout the world. With modifications and improvements, it continued to be the German army's standard sub-machine gun throughout World War 2.

The Russians took longer to find a useful, all-purpose sub-machine gun. The precursor of a long series was the *PPD* – the Degtyarev pistol machine gun of 1934. Although a little heavy, it was nevertheless an excellent weapon although their PPSh became the mainstay of the Soviet Army. Indeed, despite their fairly late start in this field, the Russians were to use far greater numbers of sub-machine guns than any other army in World War 2.

'B' for Beretta . . . 'U' for Uzi

The name of Beretta is famous throughout the world. This North Italian firm first produced a sub-machine gun the *38 A* back in 1938, designed by the talented engineer, Tullion Marengoni. It soon gained a reputation for reliability and accuracy. By 1941 – a year after Italy had entered the war on the side of the Germans – Beretta began the mass production of their sub-machine gun, the Beretta 38/42. Later versions were fitted with a smooth barrel rather than the grooved barrel of the original.

Post-war, the British began tests to replace their standard sub-machine gun – the Sten. In 1951 the *SMG L2 AI* series was introduced. Well made and well finished, this weapon has seen many modifications since its debut, and the current version is the *L2 A3*.

From the Tulle weapons factory in France came the *Mat 49* at the end of World War 2. This high quality weapon has perfect sights and an automatic safety mechanism which stops the weapon going off when not in a firing position.

After its independence in 1948 and the war against its Arab neighbours which followed, Israel began to manufacture its own arms. Major Uziel Gal conceived the *Uzi* sub-machine gun, whose manufacture began almost immediately and still goes on today. It works according to the blow-back action principle and it is manufactured by means of moulds and certain heat-resistant plastics. Most of the first *Uzis* had a very short butt, but later models adopted a metal butt that can be folded up. This weapon is also manufactured under licence in the Low Countries.

Despite all these post-war novelties, the only truly

Above A British infantryman guards a bridge armed with an assault rifle. *Inset* A short-range anti-tank weapon.

original model has been the American *Ingram*. This was destined more for the police than the armed forces. The US Army replaced the traditional *Thompson M1A1* by the *M3A1* towards the end of World War 2. Nicknamed 'the grease gun' because of its appearance, this weapon has been produced in vast quantities.

The sub-machine gun does not seem to have much of a future in today's armies. Even in South-East Asia, where it was popular for a long time – with the Chinese in Korea and the Vietnamese in Indochina – it is being replaced step by step by the Soviet-type of assault rifle. The great weakness of the sub-machine gun lies with its relatively feeble 9 mm cartridge. Nevertheless, it remains a weapon with many good qualities, cheap and easy to manufacture.

Machine guns

Together with anti-tank weapons, machine guns are part of the arsenal at group or combat section level in all the world's principal armies. It was an American, Hiram Maxim, who invented the fully automatic version, but it was an Englishman who was responsible for its massive use in conflict. As early as 1905, Lieutenant-Colonel Mac-Mahon considered that an important element in a future conflict would be superiority of fire power. During World War 1, machine guns began to be grouped together and special corps were set up.

From 1915 the machine gun dominated the field of battle to all intents and purposes. All resources and schemes were produced to make it ever more efficient and deadly. One of its most important missions was to cover withdrawals since, as was not the case with the artillery, who were unwilling to lose any guns, machine guns could be sacrificed without scruple if the situation demanded it.

In order to understand the significance of the machine gun at this period, it must be appreciated that, at the end of World War 1, the British Machine Gun Corps comprised fifty-seven battalions each with sixty-four guns each on the Western front alone.

After the *Lewis*, invented by an American, the British infantry opted for the Vickers. The French disposed of the *Saint-Etienne* and the *Chau-chat*, just as the Germans were making a lighter version of their *Maxim*. There were not many innovations between the wars, although the French did replace their *Chau-chat* with the *Chatellerault*.

The United States meanwhile was equipping itself with an excellent medium-range machine gun – the *Browning M 1917*.

After 1918 the Germans have made rapid progress and after a few trials, eventually adopted the *MG 34*, a very versatile weapon. It could be used as a medium or light machine gun, thus acting as the pre-cursor to the general purpose machine guns which were finally adopted by most armies.

Its successor, the *MG 42* was mass-produced from 1942 until the end of the war. Its lightness, coupled with its particular qualities, gave it a very high rate of firing.

The Soviet Union entered the war with a medium-range machine gun, the *Maxim*. It was soon replaced by the more modern *Gorynuov*.

The inter-war period

There were no new modifications to existing models at the end of World War 2. France, whose armaments industry needed a facelift, was forced to use Allied and German weapons during the war in Indochina, and in particular, the *MG 42*: a weapon which continued to be used by many countries after 1945. The reconstituted West German army also chose a version of the *MG 42*, adapted to the standard NATO cartridge. It is still in use under the name of *MG 3*.

Although France still has the *MG 3*, it also uses its own machine gun, the *Mat 52*. Not so in Italy, where the army has opted for the German *MG 42/49*, although between the wars the Italians used a weapon that still exists in many versions today, the *Breda model 30*.

The British now use an improved version of the *Bren*, which was first introduced in 1938. The basis of the mechanism is similar in origin to the Czech *ZB 26* machine gun. The Bren has always been a reliable and efficient weapon. As a defensive weapon, it formed the backbone of the fire barrage and it was light enough to be carried on an offensive operation.

When Britain opted for the NATO 7.62 mm ×51 calibre, the most recent Bren models were adapted to this ammunition. These modified weapons are numbered *L4 A1* to *L4 A6*.

The Soviet Union still uses the *SGM Goryunov*. Having proved its worth in many wars, it is widespread in almost all the Warsaw Pact countries. It has even been used on a grand scale by the Chinese, and the Americans had to confront many of them in Vietnam. It is manufactured in Poland, Czechoslovakia and Hungary. This machine gun has another advantage: it can be used on vehicles. In this mode, it is fixed to a special frame provided with a platform for the ammunition case and a container for collecting cartridge cases.

The other machine gun put into service by the USSR was the *RPD Degtyarev*. Manufactured in large numbers, it was the standard weapon both in the Soviet Union and its satellite countries. It is now out of date and like the *Goryunov* it is being replaced by a light automatic version of the *AK 47* assault gun, the 7.62 mm ×54R PK and PKT.

The United States produced its first machine gun, the *Browning* model 1917, during World War 1 – 43,000 being produced in one year alone. When the US army entered World War 2 the Browning was still in use and proved to be such an excellent weapon that it was used extensively in Korea. It was only replaced in the early 1960s by the new *M 60*, although the Browning *M 2* still serves as a heavy machine gun. This was also launched at the end of World War 1 and in an improved version it equips most of the combat vehicles of the US army and the British *Chieftain* tank. It is also in use in several of the Gulf States where it is mounted on a vehicle and used against relatively long-range targets.

Anti-tank weapons

When the first tanks appeared on the battlefields of World War 1 there were no light, mobile weapons for the ordinary infantryman to use in self defence. The only effective deterrent was the field gun. As the war developed, however, and the tank began to make a more conspicuous contribution to the war, the Germans found that a rifle bullet, fired at great speed, could pierce a tank's armour. Thus the first anti-tank rifle was born, though it was just a bigger version of a standard rifle, and fired an 11 mm bullet. It was

Right and *below* The French Milan anti-tank system at work.

soon found, however, to suffer from one great disadvantage: recoil.

There was little progress in this area during the years that followed the war. The *Maroszek 35* was the only exception, a Polish anti-tank rifle which made its appearance in 1935. This was instrumental in the British invention of the *Boys* – called after an officer of the same name who directed the weapon's trial programme. The trials were encouraging, penetrations of 25 mm being obtained in armour plating.

The very first models were distributed to British infantry units in 1937. Unfortunately, it soon became apparent that the tanks' armour plating had also been improved. The *Boys* was then replaced by the *Piat*. Even before the improvement in armour plating, it had become necessary to abandon the concept of the fast-moving armour-piercing projectile and to destroy tanks by means of a projectile charged with a powerful explosive. This led to the *Piat's* appearance in 1942. In spite of its drawbacks – recoil, heaviness of handling and lack of accuracy – this weapon was the first to put the infantryman on an equal level with the tank.

The Americans were working on a rocket launcher during this period. Its most celebrated manifestation was the legendary *Bazooka*, which showed its worth during the 1939-45 war. Many different versions were developed and a much more powerful model was manufactured at the beginning of the Korean war.

German copies of the *Bazooka* were made at this time. Based on the Bazookas captured from the Russian army. They were called *Ofenrohr* or, more usually, *Panzerschreck*.

A new era

As armour plating on tanks became more and more effective, simple anti-tank rifles became redundant. In Korea the Americans soon discovered that their famous *Bazooka* was no match for their opponent's weapons, even though

Above and *below* American bazookas. This anti-tank weapon proved ineffective against modern armour plating. *Inset* Two American soldiers on manoeuvres using an *M-60* machine gun.

Above A US soldier takes aim with his *M-16*. *Below* The Swedish Carl Gustav, 84 mm anti-tank weapon.

these were not of very recent design.

The authorities in Washington were thus forced to put a prototype the *3.5* rocket launcher into production. This was very effective and became standard issue in many of the world's armies. It was followed by the now standard LAW, the M72A2, in 1962.

The Soviet Union soon followed the US example and the *RPG 2* came out in 1952 – a simple but effective rocket launcher. It quickly spread to all the armies of the Warsaw Pact. Great progress was made with the recoilless principle. The British adapted this method and equipped their anti-tank units with the 120 mm *Bat*. This system causes such a violent shock that great pieces of metal are torn out of the tank.

Although Britain originated the idea, it was left to others like the Swedish Carl Gustav to perfect it. The Carl Gustav has three sighting systems: ordinary, telescopic and infra-red. Although a valuable weapon, the Carl Gustav itself has gradually been made redundant by the never-ending improvements in tank protection. It had another drawback – it was too heavy.

The Soviet equivalent is the *RPG 7*. It uses small auxiliary rockets fixed onto the projectile itself to maintain its speed after launching.

More recently the American TOW together with the French *Milan* system, has been deployed in many European armies. Both are anti-tank missiles operated and steered by wire-guidance.

Milan: the personal tank buster

It has long been acknowledged that anti-tank weapons have a useful secondary role in house-fighting or attacking strongpoints and the development of certain characteristics in modern systems like *Milan* have made them doubly effective in that role. As tanks have become tougher to crack, anti-tank power has increased. *Milan*'s warhead contains 7 kg of shaped explosive charge designed to burn right through tank armour. When it hits a hillside dugout its crushing impact is reinforced by a shock wave and sheet of flame which terrifies those it does not kill. *Milan*'s accuracy has been enhanced by a computer-controlled, wire-guided system which, it is claimed, gives a 98 per cent chance of a direct hit between 230 and 2,000 yards. The laser rangefinders and computer fire controls of the latest tanks gives them a lethal accuracy, and infantry anti-tank weapons must have a low profile and be elusive. *Milan* meets this requirement because it is launched from the prone position and is capable of being carried and operated by a single soldier. Well-trained infantry can bring it forward even into open ground swept by enemy fire, as the British did in the Falklands campaign.

Top left The *B-300* anti-tank weapon which replaced the *Law* weapons system. *Inset* The *Law 80* system. *Bottom left* The American TOW system mounted on a jeep. *Below* The *SA-7 Grail* Soviet system (anti-aircraft missile). *Top right* The *Blowpipe* ground-to-air missile. The missile's weight has made it difficult to carry and so highly unpopular with troops. *Below right* The *Milan* system used by the British army.

Milan is designed to be man-carried, but its launching pad and guidance unit does weigh 36 lb and each missile weighs 24 lb when packed – a load that even the strongest soldier will find difficult to carry for long periods. As a result, *Milan* is not used in a section anti-tank role, but in three-men teams in a battalion's company.

At Goose Green the system fulfilled British expectations and the Argentine strongpoints wilted under the combined fire with machine guns. Goose Green marked the first occasion which *Milan*'s weight of fire had been directed at clearly defined targets.

TOW

The American TOW (Tube-launched, Optically-tracked, Wire-guided) heavy, anti-tank missile, is now the US infantryman's major anti-tank weapon. It is 1,162 m long, 1.52 m diameter and 3.43 m when the wings are expanded. It has a launch weight of 20.9 kg, a range of some 500-3,750 m, and a flight speed of 1,003 km/h. Packed into its warhead is 3.9 kg shaped-charge with 2.4 kg explosive. The missile tube is attached to the back of the launch tube.

Development of the TOW began in 1965 to replace the standard US army issue 106 mm recoilless rifle. It quickly became a favourite with infantry forces and today there are three members of the TOW family: TOW, I-TOW (improved version) and the TOW-2 which is currently in production. This very modern weapon (Hughes began production of TOW-2 in 1983) has many improvements on the original TOW system, including a new warhead, a longer extendable probe which is designed to beat the new generations of tanks due to roll off the Soviet production line in the 1990s.

Certainly the future of personal anti-tank weapons lies with missiles. And these are being developed all the time. The Soviet ATGWs and the American TOWs for example no longer offer guarantees when it comes to piercing the ultra-resistant armour plating sported by the modern tank. A new generation of weapons is now in full swing, amongst them the American TOW 2.

THE PACIFIST

MOVEMENT

In the name of peace

Today, hundreds of thousands of Europeans are taking to the streets to voice their rejection of the arms race, the balance of terror and the whole system of East-West alliances. Who are the people protesting against war today and how effective is their cause?

Massive demonstration in West Germany against the deployment of missiles in Europe.

A strategy for peace

In the grim game of nuclear roulette, Hiroshima is a lasting reminder of what a future nuclear war would be like. Even today, forty years on, there are thousands of survivors who bear witness to the folly of human nature: thousands of innocent people whose only crime was to have been born in the wrong place, at the wrong time. Today the superpowers have the capacity of inflicting at least a million times more destructive power than that meted out on Hiroshima.

'If you want peace, prepare for war' has been the slogan followed by successive Western governments since 1945. But for thousands of Europeans today, especially the young, preparing for war is unthinkable lunacy. 'Peace now', is their slogan – translated by their opponents as 'better red than dead'. *Have* the governments of western Europe followed the wrong path? *Can* the politics of the smiling face and the outstretched hand succeed in disarming the most murderous of wills?

Certainly the peace movement is a reality which few governments of Western Europe can afford to ignore. Whether manipulated from outside or not, they represent an undeniable force, a popular current of feeling which springs from a sentiment people are no longer ashamed to own: fear.

To understand the scope of this phenomenon, it is necessary to know something of the groups campaigning for peace in Europe today. And to understand what they are saying it is necessary to face up to the full horror of what a nuclear war in Europe would mean.

Nuclear war: the reality

The effect of the two bombs dropped on Japan on August 6 and 9, 1945 is modest compared to the destructive power of the nuclear arsenal held by the two superpowers today. Nevertheless, they make grim reading. By 1950 – five years after the first bomb had been dropped – a total of 157,575 deaths had been recorded in Hiroshima. This was out of a civilian population of 320,000 and 40,000 military personnel. The second bomb, dropped on Nagasaki, killed 124,901 civilians out of a population of 280,000. And these figures do not include cases of severe burns, general fatigue, future cancer cases and malformation of foetuses in mothers exposed to radiation.

Modern nuclear weapons have far greater capacity to kill, wound and maim. Rumours of what such a war would mean to the civilians on the ground have, in recent years, been vivid, lurid and terrifying. But they are fears well fuelled by the facts.

In the first micro-second of a thermo-nuclear explosion, the temperature would soar from zero to 10 million degrees. If the bomb were to explode at a high altitude, the incendiary effects would increase. An explosion of 1 megatonne (1 million tonnes TNT) creates a ball of fire 1 km in diameter at sea level and 10 km at 50 km altitude.

The duration of radiation is proportionate to the power of the bomb. For 20 kilotonnes (20,000 tonnes of TNT), 1.5 seconds; for 1 megatonne, 10 seconds; and for 10 megatonnes, 30 seconds. The thermal effects are more marked when the exposure time is shortest, however. Thermal radiation causes burns of the skin of living creatures directly exposed. For 5 calories per cm^2 for one second's exposure, 2 degree burns result. There are third degree burns for 8 calories per cm^2 during the same instant. Lesions of the eyes occur at less than 1 calorie per cm^2.

Above Demonstration for peace in West Germany. The dove of peace is always very much in evidence.

The consequences of the shock wave must also be considered. They are characterised by a sudden increase in the air pressure, accompanied by very violent winds of several hundred miles per hour. A high pressure of 10 atmospheres is fatal for a human being. There is a risk of the thorax rupturing, the pelvis being crushed and multiple haemorrhage. The danger of falling buildings and people being hurled against walls must not be forgotten, since the wind caused by a pressure of 0.1 atmospheres can sweep a human being of his feet and carry him along.

At the moment of a nuclear explosion, radiation is caused by neutrons and gamma rays produced by fusion and fission reactions. Radiation acts in two ways on the body's cells: external radiation caused by penetrating rays and internal radiation from radioactive products introduced into the organism.

The effect of radiation does not only depend on the dose received but also on the localization. If there are more than 200 biological effects of absorbed radiation, the risk of death is heightened in the absence of appropriate care. If there are more than 600 effects, the outcome is fatal.

When the radioactive fall-out has settled, its actions decreases quite quickly. 80 per cent of the total dose of radiation is received on the first day, and 90 per cent in the first week. The remaining 10 per cent makes the zone dangerous for weeks or months.

One explosion of a 1 megatonne bomb 1,500 m above a town would have horrific effects. Everything would be completely destroyed within a radius of 4 km around the point of impact. The only survivors would be those in special shelters. Between 4 and 5 km, houses would collapse, half the population would be killed and the remainder wounded. Between 5 and 10 km, the most severe risk would be fire: 5 per cent of houses would catch fire and there would be the danger of this spreading. At 15 km distance, damage to dwellings would be limited, but 25 per cent of the population would be wounded.

A few examples serve to bring home the effects of a nuclear blast. If a nuclear explosion took place at night over the American city of Detroit, with about 1,500,000 inhabitants, the OTA – the Office of Technology Assessment – estimates that 47,000 would die immediately and 630,000 would be wounded. Fire and the collapse of buildings would cause a further 1,000 to 190,000 dead.

In the right atmospheric conditions, an attack launched against Europe would make an area of 250,000 km^2 – the total surface area of West Germany – uninhabitable for a month.

The peace movements
These consequences of a nuclear explosion make it easier to understand the development of the various peace movements. It is no wonder that such a terrifying arsenal has pushed hundreds of thousands into the pacifist camp. There are many peace movements, and they exist in the East as well as in the West.

The World Council for Peace
The French section of the World Council for Peace was created in 1949. Among the organizers was Frederic Joliot Curie. This organization made itself known by launching the famous 'Stockholm appeal' in March 1950 which demanded the absolute prohibition of atomic weapons.

The World Council for Peace exists mainly in the East, but it has off-shoots in Western Europe and the Third World. The positions it adopts are often remarkable. It did not condemn the Soviet invasion of Afghanistan, nor of Hungary and Czechoslovakia. Public enemy number one it considers to be 'American imperialism'.

International Confederation for Disarmament and Peace
The ICDP was founded in 1964 by representatives from Yugoslavia, France, the United States, West Germany and Britain. Fifty national and international non-aligned organizations were set up in 20 countries. With its headquarters in London, this organization has opposed NATO's nuclear strike force and the Soviet invasion of Czechoslovakia in 1968. Unfortunately, its activities are much reduced through lack of resources.

Peace movements in northern Europe
These have existed for a number of years. There are three kinds. The first were at their height in the 1950s and have since disappeared. The second are linked with a local tradition of neutrality, as in Sweden and the third were born as a result of activity of the Protestant church, as in Holland. The most famous of these is the 'IKV', the Inter-ecclesiastical Council for Peace. This movement plays a very important role.

Created in 1966 by the Catholic and Protestant churches, it sought recruits at parish level. In 1977 it launched a campaign with the slogan 'Let us aid the abolition of nuclear arms throughout the world, beginning with Holland'. This movement is now so popular that Holland and Belgium have steadfastly refused to allow NATO to station the 48 cruise missiles it wishes on their soil.

It is also due to the IKV that independent peace groups have developed in East Germany and Hungary. In 1983, for example, several unofficial disarmament demonstrations took place in Jena. More than 20 militants who took part in it were expelled and those responsible from the IKV were banned from entering the country in future.

Above Militant pacifist demonstrating against the atomic bomb.
Below Peace demonstration mounted by the Soviet authorities in Moscow in the autumn of 1983 to show the world that pacifists also exist in the Eastern bloc.

The IKV has also established fruitful contacts with Solidarnosc and representatives of Charter 77 in Czechoslovakia.

Peace movements in Western Europe
Although it is the independent leader of the new peace movement in Europe, the IKV is closely followed by other organizations grouped under the 'International Peace Communication Center'.

Peace movements in Western Europe do not oppose all weapons. Their battle is against nuclear arms, in particular intermediate nuclear missiles already in position and aimed at Europe (SS-20s) and those positioned in Europe itself (Cruise and Pershing 2).

Alongside the IKV there are other important movements:
— the Scandinavian organizations, with a definite nuclear disarmament plan for the Scandinavian countries;
— the co-ordination of the Italian peace movements, created on October 24, 1981, the outcome of a resoundingly successful demonstration of 250,000 people on that day;
— the Committee for Nuclear Disarmament in Europe, a French organization which is still in its infancy;
— CND in Britain;
— the Belgian movements;
— the West German peace movements.

Internationalising the peace movements
The spring of 1980 saw the launching of an appeal by the Bertrand Russell Foundation for Peace for a Europe without nuclear arms. The initials END (European Nuclear Disarmament) became the rallying point from then on for all the peace movements in Western Europe.

Each organization that took part in the huge demonstration in the autumn of 1981 was linked to it. The signatories of the END appeal were reunited in Rome in November 1981 and announced that July 1982 would see the first convention for a Europe without nuclear arms. This initiative was taken to co-ordinate the different national movements on an international level.

It also proposed to establish links between churches, trade unions, independent movements and political parties. Almost a thousand people were present at this meeting in Brussels. The second reunion took place in Berlin in May 1983. It was preceded by an outcry, particularly from the authorities in Moscow. However, almost three thousand people took part. The 1984 rally took place in Italy.

The neutral tendency in West Germany
West Germany occupies a separate position in the history of pacifist movements. Because of the traumas it has suffered since the beginning of the century and its awkward geographical situation, Germany has always felt itself to be in a delicate position. Its alliance with the United States does not stop it from making overtures to the East. Feelings are even more ambiguous within the population. People often opt for radical solutions in order to forget the past and put it as far behind them as possible.

Thus the growth of a vast peace movement in 1981 and the development of an official line inspired the most diverse speculations on the subject of West Germany's future in the overall Western movement. Without knowing what will emerge from this period, it is interesting to note that the same question is posed by politicians within West Germany itself.

Above Caricatures of the superpower heads of state brandished at an anti-nuclear demonstration in Bonn, West Germany.

The battle for peace enters into this debate. It unites men and women of very different political persuasions. Ecologists are to the forefront, because the struggle for peace in West Germany is the logical outcome of the struggle against the spreading of technology and all its attendant risks. However, the ecologists are not the only ones to adopt the tenets of the peace movement. Most of the political parties to a greater or lesser extent allude to it. The Church deliberately aligned itself at the time of its evangelical congress in June 1983 in Hanover.

When it entered NATO in 1955, West Germany opted for direct links with the United States to escape the menace of the Soviet Union. Today, a great majority of the population consider those links too close. A huge movement grew up in the 1960s which opposed the 'colonization' of West Germany by the United States. Even if the expression is a little strong, it contains a certain amount of truth: today West Germany is host to a multitude of nuclear weapons.

Ramstein, for example, is the largest American base in Europe, with some 6,000 personnel. And it is in the Lower Rhine valley and the Ruhr, the densest population centres, that there is the biggest concentration of missile sites and airfields, as well as industrial complexes. This is the context in which the movement opposing cruise missiles came from the Low Countries and took root at the beginning of 1981. These different organizations are in fact chasing a dream cherished over the years by succeeding generations of Germans.

They prefer to take cautious action towards disarmament which will not weaken one side at the expense of the other.

These two diverging tendencies have certain things in common, however. The unilateralists and the others are in agreement over the establishment in Europe of denuclearized zones. These would not allow the siting of nuclear missiles on their soil nor their transit across or flight over their territory.

The supporters of this view advance the argument of détente. According to them, the setting up of denuclearized zones would be a first concrete step and one that would be relatively simple to carry out. Some contact has been made in this context, for example, the talks in the Balkans between the Greek minister and Bulgaria, Rumania and Yugoslavia. Egon Bahr, a member of the German SPD, has also suggested the establishing of a denuclearized zone between the two Germanies.

The third proposal made by the pacifist movements is the freezing of existing weapons. This campaign has been developed for the most part in the United States, and nearly a million people took part in a demonstration in New York on June 12, 1983. This idea envisages a bilateral agreement between the Soviet Union and the United States to freeze trials, production and deployment of nuclear arms, of new missiles and the air forces used to launch nuclear weapons. The peace movements believe this would be the first stage in lessening the risk of a nuclear war.

The dream involves the disengagement of the two great power blocs. This proposal involves a 'purification' not only of Germany but also of the other West European countries concerned. For those Germans committed to neutrality, this would permit Europe to redefine its role. Young Germans place all their faith in this new mode of being, symbolic though it might be. It is a kind of counter-culture which rejects the division of the world.

Proposals of the peace movements

The 'peace forces' have developed a rationale over the past few years. In their estimation, the notion of imbalance in favour of the Soviet Union is ill-founded. All the peace movements believe that the siting of Pershing 2 and cruise missiles adds new momentum to the arms race, introducing technology that the enemy does not yet possess.

These organizations also have a more long-term view. They believe that the siting of new weapons in the West can only aggravate the position of the 'detainees' in the Soviet Union. In the context of increased tension, the USSR will not allow any policies of liberalization which will put its hegemony over the Eastern European countries in jeopardy. Lastly, the peace movements support two kinds of initiative for disarmament: unilateral disarmament and independent initiatives for disarmament.

The first is inspired by the belief that, whatever the risks of disarming, they are fewer than those engendered by the arms race. The second takes into account the psychological need for security felt by a great number of Europeans.

Though peace may be their aim, not all demonstrations are peaceful. Here black clad French CRS face taunts and stones from demonstrators.

EXPLAINED

'If you want peace, get to know about war'

To those who have made the study of war their business, it is not innate human aggressiveness that has produced the wars of the twentieth century and now threatens Armageddon. The causes of war are many and complex and a new generation is looking at why wars are waged. This new science of war is usually known as 'conflict studies' and aims at predicting the likelihood of future conflicts breaking out, how such a conflict might develop and how such a conflict can be contained.

The study of war as a science is still in its infancy and like all new sciences still has to find acceptance. But to Professor Gaston Bouthoul a leading exponent of these studies the choice before us is stark: either we come to understand what makes wars and learn to prevent them or we face extinction.

In an 'Open Letter to Pacifists', Professor Gaston Bouthoul says that war is too serious a matter to be left to the generals, the politicians and to those who make up the peace movement. Pacifists have traditionally, he claims, assumed that wars are made by evil people and all that is needed to prevent them is to persuade people that wars are bad. If people believed that, then there would be no war. Such a belief, argues Professor Bouthoul, is naive in the extreme. The proper way to ensure peace is to make a proper study of war. And this, says Bouthoul, involves a radical revaluation of our attitudes to both war and peace.

The proper study of war

The starting point is the assertion that wars are not some peculiar aberration, but ordinary social phenomena. This idea has met with resistance: it seems that people wish to believe that there is something mysterious, something almost mystical about war. Conflict study aims at making the facts of war plain and monitoring the alternation of war and peace in organized societies; the 'social structure of peace'; and conflict and violence and their relationship to the individual and to groups.

Today, academic research into war centres on two main areas: the 'sociology of war' and its frequency of occurrence.

The sociology of war

To Professor Bouthoul, 'the persistency of war in all times and places is evidence that it fulfills some inescapable function'. Because it is difficult to define the causes of armed conflicts, any science of war must discover the *function* wars have played in the past. And all wars it seems, including civil wars, fulfil five main functions:
1. A form of game, appealing to competitive instincts.
2. A form of speculation, establishing a connection between a risk run and a gain anticipated.
3. A form of 'reversal or consolidation of internal power and external strength'.
4. A way of changing existing structures.
5. A form of socio-economic destruction.

With the development of the tremendous destructive capacity of weapons in the twentieth century, the first of the five functions listed above, the game aspect of war, has virtually disappeared. Sport has no place in the scenario of a nuclear war, though it is not entirely absent from all modern wars as witnessed by Britain's war with the Argentine over the Falklands in 1982.

The frequency of wars

In *The challenge of war*, Gaston Bouthoul and René Carrère have succeeded in establishing that since 1740 not one year has passed without a major armed conflict.

During the period researched – 1740 to 1974 – the world saw:
— 14 years when there was one conflict only;
— 60 years when there were between two and five;
— 12 years when there were between six and ten;
— 67 years when there were between ten and twenty;
— 2 years (1863 and 1864) when there were more than twenty.

The duration of the wars is also not without interest. During the same period, 30% of the wars were resolved in less than a year; 7% lasted between one and four years and 33% lasted longer than four years.

Above Pacifist demonstrations are perhaps not the best way to preserve a lasting peace.

All these data reflects only a small part of painstaking study into all wars, past and present made in recent years. Their principal characteristics have been detailed in a questionnaire divided into two parts: the description of the phenomenon and its interpretation.

Description of the phenomenon

The sorts of questions posed by Professor Bouthoul are:
Identification (what sort of a war was it?)
Exact location (when and where did it occur?)
The protagonists (who against whom?)
Evolution of the conflict, its stages and outcomes (what and how?)
Engagement and solution (what and how?)
Numbers involved – populations, combatants, dead, etc. (how many?)
Results – internal and international (why?)

Interpretation of the phenomenon

Its terms of reference is the war itself, its motives and causes and its discernable functions. This information, it is claimed, will enable future researchers to predict the outbreak of wars and analyse their symptoms.

The ability to predict the imminence of an armed conflict, however, even if accurate, does nothing to prevent it. As Gaston Bouthoul says, we must not only 'arrive at the position where we can foresee the pressures of collective aggression of which we are the toys and victims. Just as important is the problem of diverting them or neutralising them and to find in the sociological functions of war substitutes which are less heinous. We must also re-invent methods of avoiding the possibility that the actual "balance of terror" does not degenerate into "privation of war" which will in turn create collective neuroses and suicidal tendencies'.